The Lavochkin La-5 Family

In Profile &

Erik Pilawskii

Contents

Introduction	1
La-5 Profiles	2-38
The Gor'ki Type Nomenclature Explained	39-43
La-5 Scale Line Drawings	44-75
Glossary & Abbreviations	76
Transliteration Guide	76
Appendix I: Photo Fakes	77
Appendix II: Cooling Louvres Explained	78-80
Appendix III: Gor'ki Camouflage	81-83

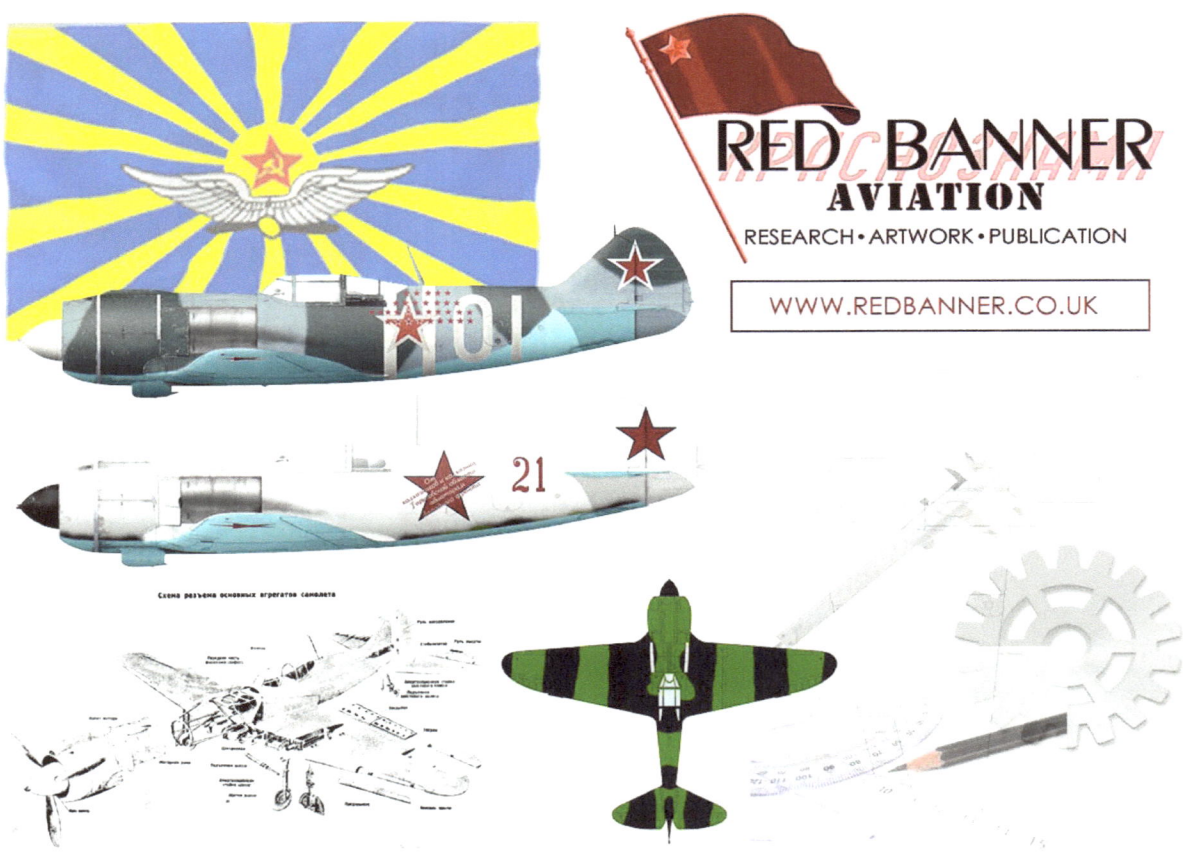

First Published 2016
ISBN 978-0-244-33598-4
Second Edition

All rights reserved. NO portion of this book may be reproduced nor transmitted in any form, nor via any possible means, to include any form or electronic or physical recording, copying or storage, without the written and certified permission of the Author.

© Erik Pilawskii
© All artwork, photographs, line drawings, schematics Erik Pilawskii

The La-5 Family

When, during the autumn of 1941, Head Engineer Mikhail Gudkov set about to convert the LaGG-3 fighter to accept the powerful M-82 14-cylinder radial engine, few could have foreseen the extraordinary transformation of the aircraft's performance and effectiveness that was to follow. Virtually at a stroke the aircraft evolved from an over-weight and under-powered fighter to one exhibiting excellent power-to-weight properties. The rugged and well designed airframe was suddenly liberated, and at last showed its full potential, indeed as its creators had intended during the inception of the I-301 programme.

Even so, early La-5 development was not without difficulty. Gudkov's prototype Gu-82 aircraft was ingenious, but it was clearly a lashed-up demonstration example and completely hand-built, and would require very considerable re-engineering for mass manufacture techniques. The design staff at Factory № 21 (at Gor'ki), under the skillful leadership of Valendinski, Alekseev, Shabanov and others, worked determinedly to rectify these matters with a new M-82 prototype on a quite severe schedule. This mad rush to introduce improved fighter aircraft for the VVS was a reflection of the extreme peril of the time. Nazi armies were but a few kilometres from Moscow, and the Red Army was certain that renewed German offensives would take place in the spring. In this kind of *survival mode* operation it was often the case that early examples of Soviet aircraft during the 1941-42 period were immature, and performance was temporarily less than envisioned. This same predicament was experienced in the early La-5 programme, the initial examples of which were designated "LaG-5" and "LaGG-5", in fact.

However, there no was denying the essential "rightness" of the La-5 design, and early troubles with both engine and airframe were rapidly rectified. By the end of 1942 the aircraft was already a war-winning machine, but it would go on to improve very much more, and by the end of the following year the -FN models were fearsome fighters, at a disadvantage to *no* enemy aircraft anywhere. It was a fitting tribute to designer Lavochkin and his staff, and the dedicated men and women who built these superb fighter aircraft.

The primary line drawings presented in this work are completed in 1:48 scale, which is common for many modellers. Detail and exploded views are scaled variously, as indicated. Notation and photographic examples have been provided to assist the modeller and historian to detect the various differences between the versions, and also amongst permutations in manufacture. These drawings are the result, it must be added, of very many years' strenuous labour, and at the time of writing certainly may be entertained as the most accurate-- and hopefully complete-- of their type anywhere.

Here, then, is the La-5 fighter family: *in Profile and Scale.*

The Gor'ki LaGG-3 M-82s

[Above, Left] The first Gor'ki built LaGG-3 M-82 protoype. The arrangement of the 'squarish' cowling was reminicent of the later unit on the La-5FN, minus the intake scoop. A contemporary LaGG-3 airframe was used for the prototype, complete with fixed tail wheel and lacking wing slats. Re-painting around the cowling is obvious, as would be expexcted, and as with all La-5 related matters, the paints in use were AMT lacquers Green (4), Black (6) and Blue (7).

The LaGG-3 M-82 № 2 prototype, April 1942. This prototype sports a confusing mixture of new and old features. The revised "Type 37" windscreen has been fitted, but not wing leading edge slats. The cowling has a 'fitted' aft edge, as on production La-5s, but the flap is unique and there is an -FN style intake along the top of the unit. The new production style oil cooler is also evident, as is the retractable tail wheel with non-bulged doors. Re-painting around the nose area, as before, is obviously in view.

Early Series LaG-5/LaGG-5

Early La-5 examples from Factory № 21 (Gor'ki) were in fact reported as "LaG-5" models, while those from Factory 31 (Tbilisi) were often referred to as "LaGG-5". A handful of these early machines were actually completed using cuncurrent LaGG-3 airframes then on the lines, such as this example. In fact, the airframe is still adorned with its Factory № 31 Production Number (a.k.a. Factory Number), which appears to be "5053". If so, this shot shows p/n 5053 during its evaluation by the NII VVS in July-August of 1942.

"White 2" is briefly seen in some 16 mm cine film taxiing out for a sortie, unit and time unknown. However, the aircraft looks suspiciously spotless, and one wonders whether this was a film prop more than a service example LaG-5? In any event, Factory № 21 style Production Numbers are seen around the tail star, which would make this model an LaGG-5. The camouflage is a bit odd in execution, and the number has been applied in a curious font, strangely located and at a 'ground angle'. All told, not a convincing appearance for a normal machine at the front.

The La-5 *Massoviy* ("Type 37")

La-5s "White 65" and "White 24" seen taxiing out in a widely published photograph. All manner of descriptions have been appended to this image, and for now perhaps it is best to say that the unit and location are still unclear. The flash at the top of the fin/rudder is a star-burst motif based upon the VVS' flag [see inset title page of this book]. "65's" cowl flap looks to be unfinished, but the forward cowl band is painted over.

La-5 "White 26" presents a rather curious appearance, and alas its unit assignment and location are unknown. The aircraft was photographed in a snowy environment, and one suspects that this image dates from the late spring of 1943. The field applied camouflage is well explained by that assumption, and most likely "26" was one of the aircraft completed at Factory № 21 with an MK-7 White livery, only, and thus in need of re-finishing for temperate conditions. The white spinner and rudder are strongly reminiscent of the Navy's 4 GvIAP, KBF and several authors have claimed that this is the operating unit.

"White 10" of the 159 IAP, summer 1943. White coloured identification devices were common amongst VMF units on the Leningrad Front, and these rudders are typical of that work. The camouflage application is curious; does this suggest the work other than Factory 21 [see Appendix III]? "White 18" was fitted with an M-82F engine [see page 15].

HSU Likholetov and HSU Zotov walking gregariously in front of "10" and "18".

The personal La-5 of Spanish volunteer Francisco Merono-Pellicer of the 960 IAP PVO, near Moscow. A number of Spanish Anti-Fascist fliers were active in the VVS, and alas their record has been somewhat rather over-looked. The inscription dedicates a presentation machine in the name of HSU Aleksandr Chekalin.

"Red 21" belonged to *Kap* Stepan Kharchenko of the 523 IAP, spring of 1943. He appears to have piloted a LaGG-3 prior to this machine bearing the same inscription, "From the Collectives and Collective Workers of the Gor'ki Region to the Fliers on the Western Front". The text was superbly picked-out in white over the star marking, showing enormous consideration and attention to detail.

"White 53" was the mount of rapidly up-and-coming 5 GvIAP ace Vitalii Popkov during the spring and summer months of 1943. The Guard's badge cannot be seen in the original photo, and is based upon a written reference by Popkov. The spinner appeared to have a small red tip.

[Right] This photograph of HSU Dmitri Nazarenko's La-5 has caused extraordinary confusion for years. The pilot to left is *Lt* K. Novikov, who so happens in this image to bear an astonishing resemblance to HSU Golubev! On the basis of a description of Golubev's "33" machine, this photo was assumed to show that aircraft. In fact, it does not, and this is indeed Nazarenko's "Red 31", 40 GvIAP, likely in the summer of 1943. The paint on the sliding canopy has mostly fallen away, as was quite common, and 14 'kill' stars are seen on the fuselage. No view is available of the cowling and spinner, and those items are a speculative reconstruction here.

[Left] An interesting, but heavily damaged, image of "White 54" reveals some curious re-painting work. The AMT-6 colour around the cowling looks to be quite fresh, and the stainless steel exhaust plate has been partly painted over. The seemingly un-painted cowl flap is most unusual for a VVS aircraft. The canopy framing is highly worn, and the fuselage star features a very thin black border.

HSU Kostilev

One of a number of airframes collected after the end of the war and "refurbished" for museum presentation was HSU Kostilev's "White 15". On display in the Leningrad *Park Pobedi*, this exhibit featured a large placard which explained that the artwork on the aircraft had been recreated with particular regard to accuracy. The claim seems plausible and reasonable, but the paints used in the museum refurbishment were glossy post-war lacquers A-26g and A-28m! The original colouration could be seen inside the cowling and cowl flap: what looked to have been AE-10 Grey applied on top of AMT-4 and -6. HSU Avdeev's Yak-9M, incidently (seen behind), was given a similarly bizarre re-painting with some type of dark grey and dark green colour, and to include a silver spinner!

The likely wartime appearance of "White 15", ca. winter 1943-44.

"The Valerii Chkalov Squadron" La-5s

During 1942 and 1943, the workers of several Collective farms in the Gor'ki region (i.e. in the great bend in the Volga above and around modern day Nizhniy-Novgorod) collected enough funds to sponsor an entire squadron of aircraft. Or, indeed, perhaps even more than one squadron-- a burgeoning number of such examples continues to surface in the photographic record. These machines were presented to the Army in the name of the district's most famous home son, Hero of the Soviet Union Valerii Chkalov -- once a local boy from Vasil'evka. As such, all of these presentation aircraft carried the inscription *Eskadrilya Valeriy Chkalov* (Valeriy Chkalov Squadron) on the port side of the fuselage. In many cases, the aircraft also carried the inscription *Ot Kokholznikov i kolkhoznits Gor'kovskoy oblasti* (From the Collectives and Collective workers of the Gor'ki region) on the starboard side.

The method of distribution of these aircraft appears to be slightly random, and is currently beyond explanation. The largest group of these aircraft appear to have been distributed to the 5 GvIAP, a notable unit chock-full of famous aces, and indeed some were deliberately given to these pilots. Most, however, were not-- they appear to have passed to any pilot in the regiment. "White 75", for example, was assigned to a young Ivan Kozhedub at a time when he was an unknown *Mladshiy Leytenant*, and in so doing passed over his famous (and brilliant) unit commander, Kirill Evstigneev (among others). Furthermore, a large number of these aircraft passed to both the 159 IAP and 4 GvIAP KBF in small groups, while the remainder were dispersed amongst several other units individually. A number of "Chkalov" examples appear to have been delivered in factory applied winter finish, which in turns suggest that these must have been received during the winter of 1942-43 (likely in 1942; the use of MK-7 White lacquer was abandoned during 1943). Some examples sport an appliqué white finish, these suggesting that such would have been delivered even earlier, *before* the winter months of 1942. The full story, and the relevant details of where and when these delightful aircraft were delivered, remains unknown.

(port side fuselage)   (starboard side fuselage)

Although similar, the precise font and script types were not always identical. These are typical examples of the various "Chkalov" inscriptions.

"White 66" of the 159 IAP. The photo caption is dated 1944, and while this is just possible, it seems a less likely timing than 1943. The retention of AMT-4/-6/-7 colouration was known during 1944, but this was quite rare, and in any event this example does not exhibit wear and distress to the surface suitable for one or two years' service.

The "Valeriy Chkalov" La-5 of Evgeniy Tsiganov, 4 GvIAP KBF. The colouration of the numeral and text on this example has been a vexation for years. On balance, it does not seem to be any permutation of white, dirty or otherwise. Many possibilities could be explained by the image, but perhaps a yellow colour is the most straightforward of those. Art profile experimentations using a possible "locally sourced" red colour proved to be rather unconvincing.

[Left] "White 84" was extensively photographed at an exhibition of captured enemy aircraft held at Rechlin, Germany, during the autumn of 1943. The lack of information regarding this example is disheartening, being so delightfully marked with 'lightning bolts' on both sides of the fin/rudder.

"White 99" of the 4 GvIAP during the summer of 1943. *StLt* Bichkov is in view along with two other unidentified Naval pilots. The "Chkalov" inscription on "99" shows a feature common to many such dedication examples, in that the text was painted in red, but where it crossed over the red star the letters were carefully picked-out in white, so as to be visible on the aircraft.

This particular aircraft is thought to have belonged to *Gen* Savitskiy of the 3 GIAK headquarters flight, even though there are no known photographs showing him in the cockpit of "60", while there are images of other, younger, pilots in it with the engine running! Be that as it may-- and indeed the aircraft might have been shared by several pilots-- the appearance of this example is at least well documented. The "Chkalov" inscription appears to have been white in colour, but either older (worn) than the numeral, or having been applied with slightly off-white paint.

It would seem that only a few "Chkalov" examples were delivered to the 240 IAP during the summer of 1943, and this particular aircraft, "White 75", went to a neophyte pilot by the name of Ivan Kozhedub. It was with this very machine that he would open his account on 6 July (Ju 87), and indeed subsequently to score all of his kills during the second half of the year.

[Right] HSU *PodPolk* Aleksey Sashenko of the 180 GvIAP with his "Chkalov" La-5. Alas, the quality of the photograph is poor, with damage to the print affecting the right and left sides of the full image. Some authors have claimed that this might be an early La-5F model, noting a suspicious round 'blob' feature allegedly on the cowling.

HSU Ivan Sytov's "White 18", 5 GvIAP, summer 1943. While most were not, this "Chkalov" example does appear to have been an "-F" model "Type 37", again suggesting most strongly that not all of these presentation aircraft were completed simultaneously. The inscription text was not picked-out over the star, and again therefore not likely to have been a red colour; as with other such examples, it is shown here in yellow.

The appearance of "Chkalov" number "20" has been much debated over the years, and indeed no consensus has yet been reached on this matter. The fact that the text has not been picked-out where it crosses the star marking would suggest that its was evident over that insignia, and thus that its colour was not red. The numeral is equally mysterious, and its colour does not seem to agree with either the star's nor the inscription's colour. "20" is shown here in A-7 Blue primer; further possibilities for this item abound.

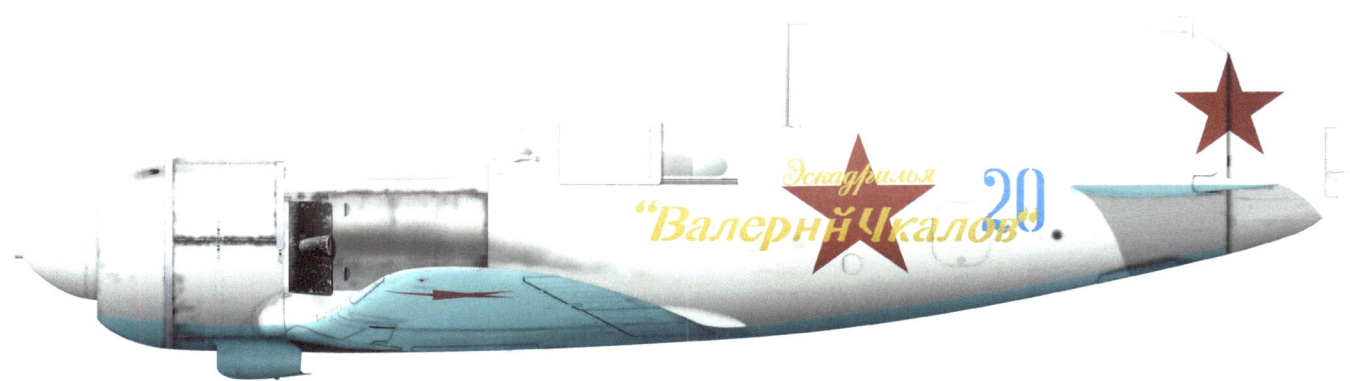

Two delightful winter camouflaged "Chkalov" examples which have previously been identified as being in service with the 21 IAP during the winter of 1942-43. The timing is almost certainly correct, but the unit attribution is simply not currently confirmed. The number "42" looks to have been applied in red, although worn or not particularly well executed, whereas "92" has the same mysterious appearance as "20" (see above), and is here shown with an identical colouration.

[Right] Two well used "Chkalov" La-5s seen during the spring of 1943, unit and location unknown (some sources suggest the 5 GvIAP). The aircraft in the foreground might be "88", which is known in another image to have flipped on its back in a ground-loop mishap. Behind is our profile subject "Red 58" with a very worn winter appliqué. The "Chkalov" inscription has been delightfully picked-out in white over the star marking.

[Left] *Chkalov* "White 69" of an as yet unknown regiment, date unknown. The thin white border around the national stars is quite interesting, perhaps foreshadowing the adoption of such markings as the standard insignia during 1943 (albeit with thicker borders). When applied, these thin outlines were no doubt a replacement for the original thin black trim, and would surely have been a decoration.

The Early La-5F ("Type 37")

From the same image showing "White 10" [see page 5]. The various details of the finish-- no fuselage star, "F" badge high on the cowling, Black camouflage demarcation on fin leading edge, etc-- may suggest manufacture at another factory than № 21 (Gor'ki).

Another La-5F "Type 37" of the 3 GvIAP KBF. This Naval regiment seems to have received a significant number of such La-5 models during the spring of 1943. "91" features the usual white spinner and rudder of this unit, and also some unusually small national star insignia.

"White 81" has been persistently associated with Petr Kal'sin of the 5 GvIAP, during 1943. This attribution stems from a photograph which shows Kal'sin standing near the aircraft; while previously seen as significant, in modern research we have learned by now that such coincidental placement is meaningless. The photo caption correctly identifies "81" as an La-5F, and as a result many profiles invariably depict this machine as a Type 39, which it clearly is not. The tactical numeral and national stars were not applied in the most careful manner.

The La-5F *Massovii* ("Type 39")

Soon after the introduction of the M-82F engine the La-5 programme adopted the new "Type 39" airframe to compliment it. The cut-down rear fuselage and cockpit changes were obvious, but internal modifications were also applied. Known inevitably as the *massovii* La-5F (as it represented the bulk of series manufacture), the majority of these aircraft were finished when built in AMT-4/-6/-7 colouration. Kpt Aleksei Maksimenko's "White 31" was a rather typical such example, showing the classic Gor'ki factory finish. No "F" badge can be seen on the cowling-- which would have been virtually standard on factory work-- and the cockpit sliding hood had been removed, both observations suggesting some modification or field work.

An La-5F seen in service with the 4 GvIAP KBF, autumn 1943. The white trim on the rudders seems to have been a bit worn, on which the "F" badge and Production Number have been carefully masked out.

"White 77" was seen in Germans hands having been captured under unknown circumstances. The camouflage application is a bit odd, possibly suggesting field re-painting or even an early example from Factory № 99. Be that as it may, this La-5F sports a white rudder and spinner, highly reminiscent of VMF regiments around Leningrad.

[Left] "White 48" seen is a rather flesh looking appearance, and clearly not wearing Gor'ki style camouflage. Indeed, this simplified application is usually associated with Factory № 381's work (Moscow), and likely that is the source of this example. The "F" badge is quite prominent on the cowling but very faint on the rudder, and the stainless steel exhaust plate has been painted over.

Towards the end of the year 1943, Soviet aviation factories began to employ a new camouflage finish which had been suggested by the NKAP. Two new upper surface colours were specified-- AMT-11 Grey-Blue and AMT-12 Dark Grey-- and indeed even a pattern of application was mooted, this via an "official" diagram. As one might expect, this pattern was only loosely followed (when it was at all), but the new colouration did replace the earlier Green/Black finish for fighter manufacture. "White 66" looks to have been finished at the factory in one of these "NAKP Template" schemes, and indeed of which it was very much a classic example.

[Left] The Lavockin Bureau designed "F" badge, applied to the cowling, and sometimes the rudder, of La-5F models [see page 41].

Many La-5F aircraft had a service life which spanned the introduction of a new paint colour system, and in that process acquired many weird and wonderful field applied schemes. "White 32" was a fairly typical example of this field work, in which a moderate attempt was made to *roughly* replicate the NKAP Template pattern. The rear fuselage upper/lower colour demarcation "ramp" feature was unusually straight on this machine.

"White 45" is thought to have been the personal mount of HSU Ivan Tsapov while with the 3 GvIAP KBF during 1944. The camouflage is unremarkable, and might have been either a factory scheme, or a well applied field re-painting job.

"White 81" was photographed at Tula during 1944, but its regimental ownership remains unknown. It is again a rather typical looking La-5F ca. 1944. The numeral "81" features a lovely thin red outline.

This still was taken from some 16 mm cine film which depicted a regimental line-up readying for action. All of the machines in view were La-5F models wearing 1944 style AMT-11/-12/-7 colouration, save ironically for the lone La-5FN model in the foreground. Despite being the newer version, this aircraft was still wearing an AMT-4/-6/-7 livery-- a most curious situation, indeed! All of the -F models demonstrate field re-painting work, and "82" features some delightful trim on its rudder.

The following profiles depict "30", "24", "08" and "82" in physical order, from foreground aft.

[Left] This famous La-5F, "White 11", has been very widely profiled, but following a thorough examination of the photo, many new details have been revealed. The camouflage is certainly a field applied job with many odd features. Of these, the wing root application to starboard of AMT-12 is most unusual, and is explained by the replacement (or original and un-repainted?) cowling piece, this still in AMT-4/-6 colouration. Late war style outlines ("Victory type") have been added to the original star markings, resulting in a poor fit over the fin/rudder. The inscription *Mongol'skii Arat* was applied in red, and the numeral "11" has been partly trimmed with this colour as well (likely the original part of the scheme).

[Left] This superb image was shot by US Army Air Force personnel on Kodak monochrome slide stock during Operation Frantic (1944). "White 18" was re-painted with a single colour upper surface scheme of AMT-11, and the rear fuselage upper/lower colour demarcation was exceedingly 'low'; in fact nearly invisible. Inexplicably, the national star on the fin/rudder was very nicely executed, while that on the fuselage is so disastrous that words fail. The cowling is not in view and the presence of the "F" badge is speculative.

"White 04" was photographed by German personnel having been captured after coming down behind enemy lines. The national stars have been applied in a rather 'wonky' and unco-ordinated manner, as have the fin stripes and the lighting bolt. The photograph's caption reveals the German flair for VVS aircraft recognition-- even as late as 1944-- by identifying the subject as a "Jak-6".

This La-5F shows one of the more curious field applied AMT-11/-12 schemes, examples of which were seen so regularly during the early months of 1944. The national stars have remained as plain red types, which is most unusual (albeit attractive). A white flash was added to the fin/rudder, and the numerals *may* (the film is in poor condition, so one cannot be certain on this point) feature a kind-of 'pin-stripe' centre trim.

HSU Gal'chenko

HSU Leonid Gal'chenko was notable for his series of delightful cat adorned LaGG fighters while serving with the 145 IAP. After having moved to the command flight of the 259 IAD, that tradition seems to have been revived on his personal La-5F. The first image of this aircraft [Right] shows a newly re-painted machine, smartly turned out for the photo with little wear in evidence. A simple AMT-4/-6/-7 scheme was applied in broad 'bands', and as usual for his aircraft, no tactical number was seen. His personal cat emblem adorned the fin/rudder, along with a remnant of an "F" badge above. The radio mast and aerials have been removed.

[Left] Gal'chenko's La-5F at an unspecified later date. Untold numbers of profiles have been made of this aircraft and, seemingly without exception, the scheme has been interpreted as AMT-11/-12/-7. One wonders, really, how this could be so? The machine is *quite obviously* wearing the same finish as seen in the earlier image, only now with some additional AMT-6 appliqué, tail stripe, award devices and spinner trim! A diabolical light reflection has made it impossible to determine if 'kill stars' may be seen on the white field below the cockpit, but surely such would have appeared there if not at the time of this image, then shortly thereafter.

La-5F Aircraft of the Aces

The famous La-5F of HSU Ivan Kozhedub, early 1944. With the abandonment of MK-7 White winter finish, some units sought a seasonal replacement colouration during the winter of 1943-44. Naval units of the time occasionally made use of AE-10 Grey, while the 240 IAP (later 178 GvIAP) specifically described their own scheme using a 50/50 mixture of AMT-11 and -12, as seen here. The dedication inscription refers to the funds for the aircraft donated by Collective Farm named for V. V. Konev.

"White 10" has long been associated with HSU Aleksandr Pavlov of the 41 GvIAP, but in fact, to date no *absolute* confirmation of his ownership of this example has emerged. Be that as it may, this example sports a delightful fin/rudder trim and stripe, with the trim tab picked out carefully. The scheme is generic enough to be either a factory or a careful field application.

This aircraft, "White 20", has a much mooted history-- both written and in profile. It is generally accepted to have photographed with the 21 IAP during the summer of 1944, and clearly from the score below the fuselage was the mount of an ace pilot. *Which* pilot, alas, is still unknown. The aircraft was finished with a casually applied NKAP type field scheme, and likely featured a red spinner.

To the great frustration of this author, HSU Vitalii Popkov's famous "White 01" is still, to this day, pathologically depicted as an La-5FN model. It was not; clearly, "01" was an **La-5F**, as shown here. Ironically, Popkov's actual La-5FN was correctly identified and published in Western literature as early as 1968 [see page 33]; apparently, however, without much notice. All manner of rather absurd colouration and markings details have been applied to this example over the years, to include French style 'blob' camouflage, "yellow" numerals and stripes, additional text inscriptions and port side nose artworks. All of these such "interpretations" are unverified, or simply wrong. "White 01" was finished with a field applied AMT-11/-12 scheme and featured variously white (some worn, some newer) details. An area of AMT-6 remained below the aft canopy section.

HSU Petr Belyasnik's "White 40" presents the researcher with a formidable task of interpretation, despite the fact that four images (at least) exist of this machine. The scheme is obviously field applied, but with areas of both sharp and soft edged colour demarcation in view. Indeed, its ad-hoc nature suggests more than one painting episode, and in fact areas of the original AMT-4/-6 colouration are seen on the fin and exhaust flap. A small repair or patch has been applied aft of the stainless steel plate, which itself has been painted over. The strangely thick black borders around the star markings are likely remnants of the original camouflage, having been masked out during refinishing. "F" badges have been carefully applied to the cowling and rudder tip, in stark contrast to the 'casual' nature of the rest of the scheme. The inscription records the dedication of the aircraft to Kpt Belyasnik, personally.

The "Valeriy Chkalov Squadron" La-5F

Only a single La-5F *massovii* "Chkalov" examples is known currently, this being "White 20", above. The aircraft has been suggested to be in service with the 159 IAP, but no confirmation of the attribution has been forthcoming. The scheme is an unremarkable AMT-4/-6/-7 application, and could have been from any of the three La-5 factories.

Post-War Presentation La-5F

"White 92" was interestingly photographed shortly after the War as an exhibit dedicated to the victory over Fascist Germany. The reference photograph caption indicates that the aircraft was situated in Tallin, likely during 1945.

The finish in view was a field applied NKAP type pattern, and presumably that which it carried during the war. The airframe generally looks to have been cleaned, and the stainless steel exhaust plate has been painted over. Both a Guard's emblem and a Red Banner badge have been applied to the starboard fuselage, these followed by a significant explanatory text, which reads in full:

"In this aircraft Hero of the Soviet Union Guards Captain Kravtsov destroyed over the city of Leningrad 31 Hitlerite enemies."

Early La-5FN "Type 39"

This early La-5FN was photographed in service with the 32 GvIAP at Kursk, summer 1943.

"White 58 seen at Factory 21, May 1943. The aircraft is freshly turned out, likely before any testing has started, and oddly features the later style diamond type "FN" badges.

[Left] "White 57" in service with an unknown regiment, 1943. The spectacular red nose is evident, as is the delight of the as yet unidentified pilot below the wing. Despite being an early La-5FN example, "57" has the later diamond "FN" badge on the cowling and rudder.

The La-5FN *Massovii*

"White 01" was shown having come to grief after a crash landing in front of Thunderbolts of the 225 IAP KBF during 1945. The operating unit of this example is still unknown. The finish is no text-book example of the NKAP style, albeit one of such type, and a diamond "FN" badge was applied to the cowling and rudder.

This very attractive machine is thought to have belonged to N. Panev of the 171 IAP, autumn 1944. Quite interestingly, this example features early style round "FN" badges and late style VVS national insignia ('Victory' types; thin red outline); a rather odd combination.

"White 10" was photographed in service with the 3 GvIAP KBF at Lavansaari aerodrome on the Leningrad Front, summer 1944. The regiment's trademark white spinner and rudder trim are clearly in view, as is a very nice NKAP style scheme.

"White 21" is known from a TASS image which circulated briefly during the 1960s and 70s. It depicts a fairy typical La-5FN, and features a flash on the fin/rudder. The poor quality of the photo makes a colour analysis impossible, and the trim has been shown here in yellow.

Another 159 IAP Lavochkin sporting the unit's typical white rudder. The camouflage is clearly field applied, and in this case with ugly hard edged demarcations; most ungainly. This is in stark contrast to the lovely rudder trim tab and star outline, and one wonders how such an appearance came about on "White 36"?

"White 81" of the 3 GvIAP KBF, summer 1944. Many Soviet regiments-- both Army and Navy-- used white trim heavily along the Leningrad Front, becoming something of an ad-hoc identification marking.

"White 95" was a typical La-5FN example, and was photographed at the NII VVS during the summer of 1944. Of note are the late style national star markings.

A "*Mongol'skii Arat*" marked fighter of the 2 GvIAP, 1944. Many of the La-5FNs of this regiment wore the inscription in red (as here), and also featured variously completed white cowlings and/or spinners.

Three-digit tactical numbers were a considerable fad in some VVS regiments throughout the war, and indeed these seemed to come into, and out of, fashion regularly. "White 180" was another 2 GvIAP "*Mongol'skii Arat*" La-5FN, and featured a very attractive white nose. [see photo page 32]

This heavily sooted La-5FN was photographed in service with the 159 IAP along the Leningrad Front, autumn 1944. The NKAP style scheme might be field applied, but is not especially unusual in execution, and the regiment's trademark white spinner and rudder are clearly in view.

[Right, Above] The date, location and ownership of this *utterly* spectacular machine are, alas, currently unknown. "Red 42" sports some of the most intricate and delightful artwork seen on any Lavochkin fighter of the GPW era. The award device inside of the modified national star is an Order of Lenin badge, this superimposed with a numeral "1" (likely indicating the first such award on the part of the aircraft's pilot, who is seated in the cockpit). The nose and cowling are obscured, but the tip of the spinner (at least) looks to be white, and here has been completed entirely in that colour. Moreover, the star on the fin/rudder is a lovely 'Kremlin Type' 3d marking. Considerable wear and exhaust staining demonstrate that this aircraft was certainly in service and not some kind of photo opportunity creation.

La-5FN Aircraft of the Aces

Twice HSU Kiril Evstigneev was one of the most formidable of all Soviet wartime aces, and a superb leader of men. "White 14" likely dates from October 1944, when Evstigneev assumed command of the 178 GvIAP. The 'chevron' device was most unusual, and the inscription to port is a dedication from the Collective workers of the V.V Konev farm.

"White 15" is the fairly well known mount of HSU Petr Likholetov, summer 1944, 159 IAP. Both images of this aircraft [lower Left; lower Right] have been widely published, and many profiles of this La-5FN are known. The text reads "For Vaska and Shora", which is a personal tribute whose significance is known only to Likholetov.

HSU Aleksandr Maiorov's La-5FN "White 70", 2 GvIAP, date unknown. This machine is adorned with the inscription "*Mongol'skii Arat*" despite the fact that it was not serving with a Mongolian regiment. This inscription became very popular indeed during the war, perhaps in the same manner as the *Valeriy Chkalov* dedication before it. In contrast to "White 180" [see page 29], the inscription in this case is surely not red in colour, and has been interpreted here as yellow. Maiorov's *white* flight boots constitute an insidious fashion crime.

[Left] An impressive collection of aces is seen in this shot, with HSUs Pavlov and Lobanov standing in front of "White 70", and who is thought to be HSU Sementsov in the cockpit. This La-5FN is yet another "White 70" machine associated with Sementsov, although there exists a photograph of Lobanov patting the 'heart' emblem. Even so, the red heart emblem is mentioned by Sementsov, and likely this was indeed his aircraft.

At last, a solution might have been found as regards the ownership of this delightful La-5FN. Most researchers agree that "White 71" did belong to the 254 IAP, and the date is certainly in the latter half of 1944. Recently, a photo of HSU Nazimov of the 254 IAP has materialised showing him next to his La-5F "White 17". That machine features a very similar arrangement and number of 'kill stars' as compared to "71", and Nazimov a very striking resemblance to the pilot in "71". It seems extremely likely that "White 71" was indeed Nazimov's personal La-5FN.

HSU *Kpt* K.S. Nazimov of the 254 IAP with his La-5F "White 17", spring 1944.

A close-up of the pilot in the cockpit of La-5FN "White 71".

As seen previously, Popkov's famous "White 01" was his *La-5F* aircraft; "White 75" was his **La-5FN**. Many details of these machines have become mixed over the years, such as the Guard's badge on the nose of "75" ("01" had no such marking). This photo [Left] of Popkov with "75" is part of a series of official TASS images of Popkov taken during the autumn of 1944, and there is also a small bit of 16 mm *cine* film depicting the aircraft, likely taken during the same visit. The finish seems to be a perfectly normal NKAP style scheme, but with a very odd aft colour demarcation 'ramp', perhaps suggesting some local re-painting.

La-5FNs at *Tri Duby*

For many years the main reference for Western readers regarding the appearance of La-5FN fighters were gleaned from a number of photographs of these aircraft in service with the 1 Czechoslovak IAP at *Tri Duby* (Three Oaks) airfield in September 1944. Ironically, the appearance of these machines could not have been farther from the typical example! For reasons unknown, virtually all (or, in fact, all indeed) of the Lavochkins photographed at *Tri Duby* were re-painted in the most extraordinary ways, deviations from the usual NKAP style finish being at times almost total. The following six profiles (pages 33-34) demonstrate some of these curious schemes.

La-5FNs of the 1 Czech SAD

This example is known from a famous in-flight shot which shows aircraft of the 1 Czechoslovak Mixed Air Division (1 Cz SAD) during 1945. "White 3" has an unusual band around the fuselage, and one suspects this was used to omit one of the original digits of the tactical number. As with so many Czech Lavochkins, the spinner has been coloured in their own unique style, in this case with red.

Another 1 Cz SAD La-5FN, "White 53". This aircraft had a nice NKAP style finish and a spiral stripe on its spinner.

"White 95" demonstrates a rather elaborate NKAP type finish and a delightful red and white spinner. The tactical numerals, alas, have not been applied with great care nor aplomb.

La-5FNs In Post-War Czechoslovak Service

During the summer of 1945 the various Czechoslovak air units remained under the auspices of the Soviet VVS, and therefore red star national insignia were still carried. "White 17" was photographed during this period, when many Czech markings features started to appear, but as yet no Czech insignia. The lightening bolt feature on the nose-- so typical of La-5s and La-7s in later Czech service-- can be seen, along with a painted spinner. The star on the fuselage is quite odd, being small, applied quite low and of curious border thickness and geometry.

The appearance of "White 68" has been gleaned from a very poor photograph, and thus the profile here must be regarded as partly reconstructive in nature. That said, "68" is demonstrative of a whole species of La-5FNs in early Czechoslovak service in which existing stocks of AMT-11 lacquer were used to complete a uniform (or so) upper surface finish, this often with incomplete coverage and obvious problem areas. New serial codes and new paint finishes were specified in January 1946, and thereafter the new olive coloured finish was often applied. This aircraft shows all of these imperfections, and clearly the cowling had originally been painted in AMT-12.

[Right] Another example of these "interim" scheme La-5FNs in Czech service. AMT-11 has been applied with variable success over the original camouflage.

Luftwaffe Test La-5 Examples

[Left] This La-5F is shown during its examination and flight testing at Rechlin, summer 1944. Some researchers of Luftwaffe matters have questioned if the swastika marking on the tail might have been removed from this image? The artist examined this photo in detail, and on balance it seems not to have been modified, although an expert in image manipulation might have done so without detection. Be that as it may, the contrasting paints on the aircraft make for a fascinating comparison, areas of RLM 76 being prominent along the aft fuselage and tail. The all-yellow nose is, admittedly, somewhat attractive.

"White 21" is known from a series of *extremely* poor photographs, and as a result this profile must be regarded as partly reconstructive in nature. The aircraft was seen at Rechlin under flight examination testing, and the ad-hoc nature of the scheme in view-- retaining most of its VVS livery-- was unusual for the Luftwaffe. It may have been the case that "White 21" fell into German hands in good condition, and that testing was expedited thereafter. Be that as it may, the spiral spinner detail is certainly of German origin, and the fin featured a large *swastika* (here omitted).

A Short History of La-5 Development and the Gor'ki "Type" Nomenclature

When development began in earnest on the new LaGG-3 M-82 prototypes at Factory № 21, in Gor'ki (now renamed Nizhnii Novgorod), the current manufacturing programme at the factory was for the "Type 31". To the rest of the world -- including the Soviet government and bureaucracy-- this was the "LaGG-3" aircraft; but the Gor'ki staff had no interest in outside designations. Their own system was to number each aircraft type which they had been tasked to build consecutively. Therefore, the LaGG-3 was in fact the 31st construction programme launched by Factory № 21, and thus the "Type 31". No further nomenclature was needed; nor even welcome.

In the Lavochkin programme at Factory № 21-- and not, it must added, in other designers' programmes built there such as the Polikarpov I-16-- the "Type" designation referred to the aircraft's *structure*; that is to say, the airframe. The "Type" nomenclature *did not* make reference to, nor include, the motor type, or at the very least the sub-type of the motor. Ironically, development of the La-5 began at the very moment that airframe changes were being implemented on the LaGG-3 (Type 31), but since Gor'ki was now assigned to develop the La-5 (development of the LaGG-3 had been reassigned to Factory № 31 at Tbilisi), all subsequent LaGG airframe enhancements were applied without any change in Type identification.

In this confusion, a standard airframe with stipulated details was agreed between the Factory № 21 staff and the NKAP in Moscow, this receiving the Gor'ki designation "Type 37". The Type 37 airframe was similar to the latest LaGG-3 enhancements, with the removal of the outer wing section fuel cells and landing light, and included leading edge slats, retracting tail wheel with flush doors, internally balanced rudder, and also featured the new flat windscreen. However, the staff at Factory № 31 proposed an "LaG-5" model, which would consist of a current LaGG-3 airframe completed with the new La-5 (Type 37) engine and cowling. A number of such hybrids were indeed built, although not in large numbers. Simultaneously, and likely reacting to the developments at Tbilisi, the staff at Factory № 21 also built a number of hybrid machines using LaGG-3 airframes currently on the prodduction lines. These were usually reported by the staff at Gor'ki as the "LaGG-5", but also at times as the "LaG-5" as well. Virtually none of these hybrid aircraft seems to have had leading edge wing slats, and they all had the LaGG-3 airframe's rounded windscreen.

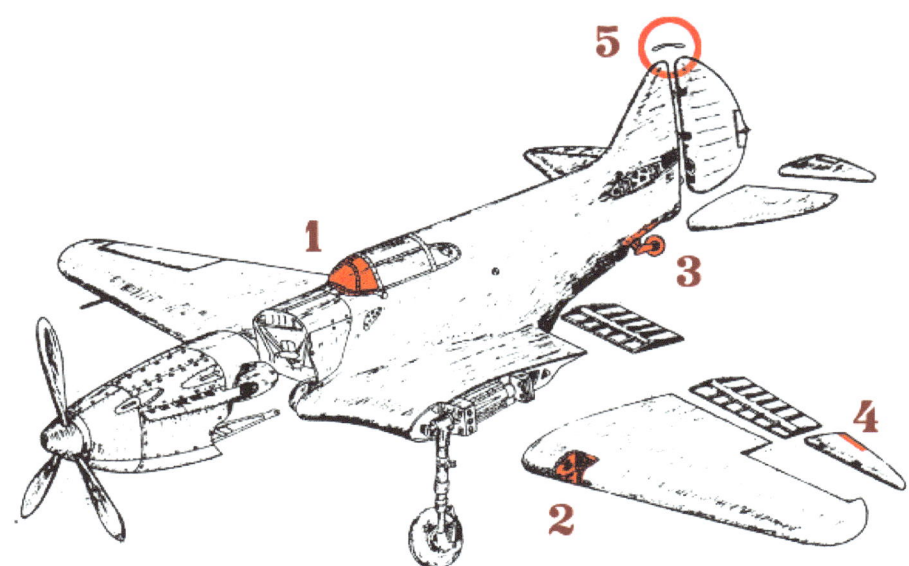

Contemporary features of the Type 31 built at Gor'ki, and therefore could seen on hybrid LaG-5 and LaGG-5 aircraft, included: 1. curved windscreen; 2. leading edge landing light; 3. fixed tail wheel; 4. cockpit adjustable aileron trim tab (port only); 5. some examples still had external rudder balance horns.

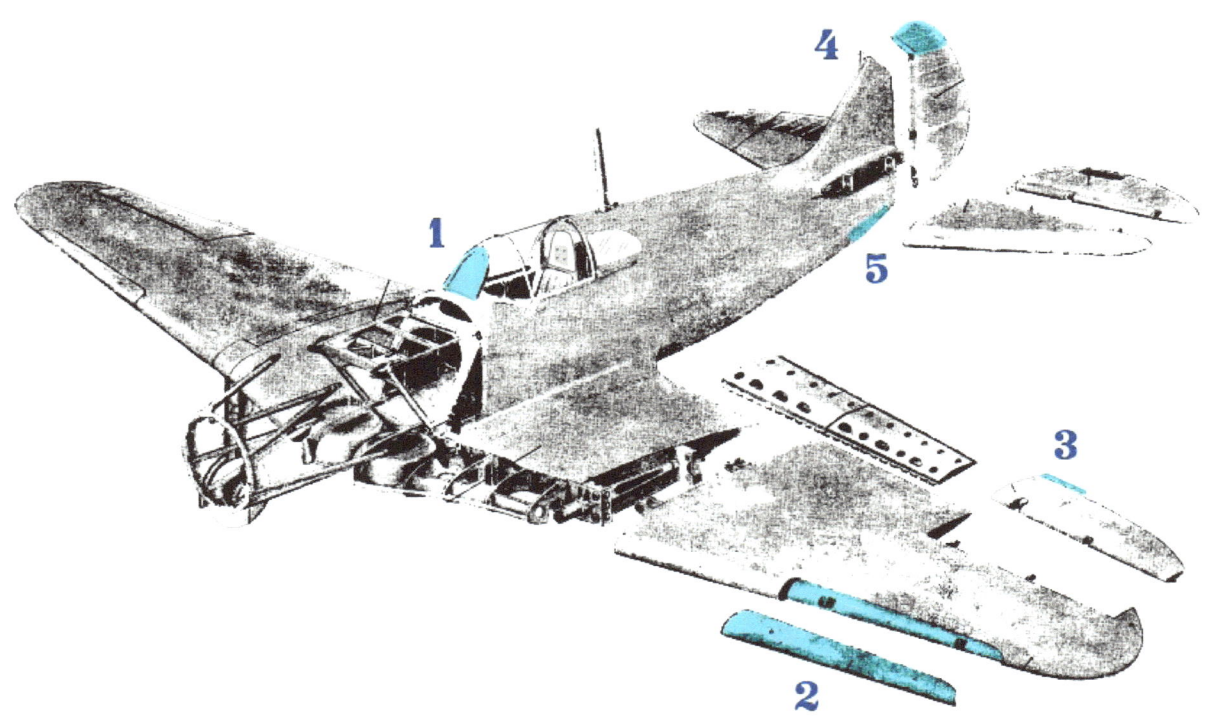

The Type 37 airframe for the La-5 programme. This was to incorporate several new features, including: 1. a flat windscreen (no armour-glass yet fitted); 2. leading edge wing slats; 3. ground adjustable aileron trim tabs (both sides); 4. internal rudder balancing; 5. retractable tail wheel with flush doors

Factory № 21 built an unknown number of these LaG-5 (or LaGG-5) aircraft (20 during June, 31 during July), and even in series. In a report during August 1942 to Stalin, P. Ya. Fedrovi mentioned both the LaG-5 and LaGG-5 *by name*, and indicated that examples of the LaGG-5 2nd and 3rd Series, specifically, were allocated to the 434 IAP. Ironically, examples of the La-5 *massovii*-- the standardised, mass-production model Type 37-- were also being built at Gor'ki alongside the hybrids. Authors Vestsik and Vrany, in their fine **MBI La-5** work, identified that the start of La-5 *massovii* (Type 37) production began with Series 8; this might well be true, and therefore most of the preceding models were most likely LaG-5 and LaGG-5 hybrids built in abbreviated Series.

Back in Moscow, the central bureaucracy became increasingly frustrated with Factory № 21's unique naming conventions. Indeed, this became such a problem that the NKAP issued Order № 683 which insisted that henceforth designations such as "Type 37" would not be used, and that all LaGG-3 radial modifications and developments were to be named "La-5". Quite hilariously, the staff at Gor'ki responded three days later by informing the NAKP that further "La-5" development would therefore be known as the "Type 38"! This petulant nomenclature is, in fact, directly confirmed: during March 1943 the LII tested two La-5FN prototypes, including p/n "38210531"; a Gor'ki "Type 38"!

When the new and more powerful M-82F engine was at last cleared for mass production, examples of this motor were immediately made available to the La-5 programme. Not especially interested in design suffixes (as Soviet designers usually were not), Lavochkin at least agreed that the model would be designated the "La-5F", specifically referencing the new engine. These -F engines were applied to existing Type 37 machines on the production lines, and therefore to the staff at Gor'ki their designation was the same-- these were, after all, Type 37 *airframes*. Lavochkin's staff designed a smart new "F" badge to be placed on the cowling of models with the M-82F, which were otherwise indistinguishable from aircraft with the M-82A.

At the same time, work was well advanced on an improved La-5 airframe with a cut-down rear fuselage and other modifications. The new structure acquired the inevitable Gor'ki designation of "Type 39", and this became the agreed standard with the NKAP for revised production, and to include the use of the M-82F engine by default. The new model became known everyone save for the Factory № 21 staff as the La-5F *massovii*, being the intended standard with the -F engine for series manufacture.

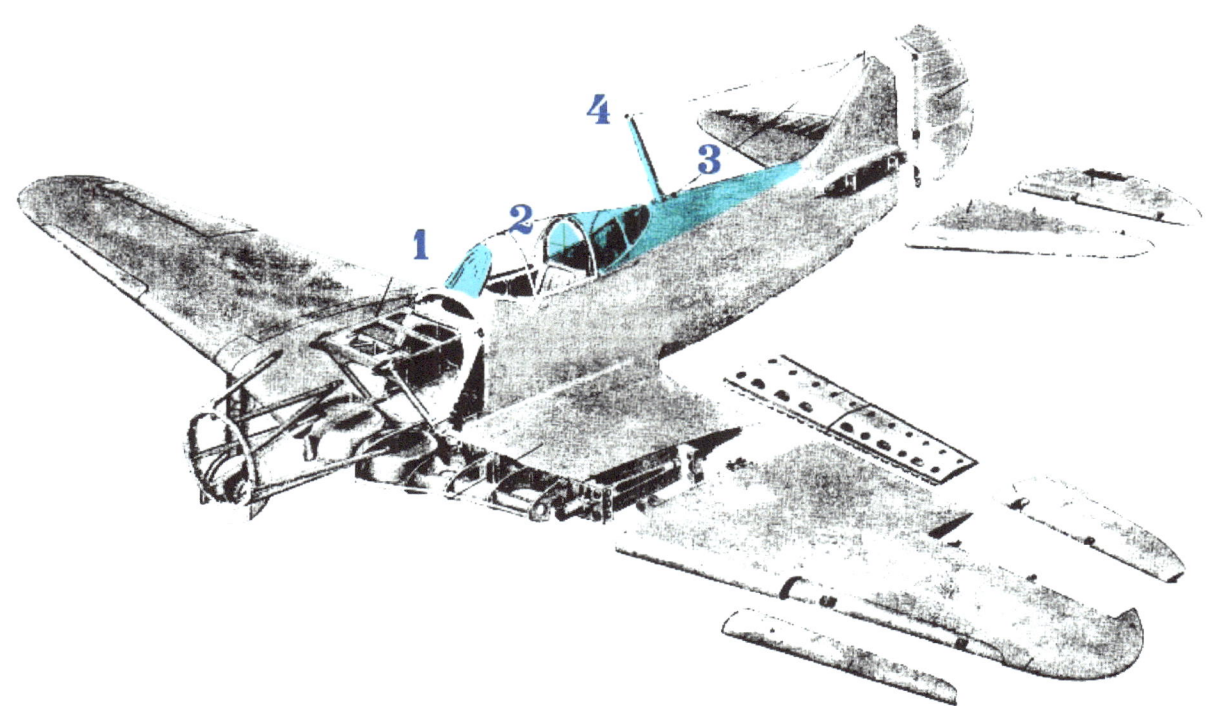

The new Type 39 airframe with cut-down fuselage. The main features of this new model were: 1. 58 mm armour-glass windscreen; 2. 68 mm armour-glass panel behind the pilot's head; 3. cut down rear fuselage turtledecking; 4. new radio mast (inclined forward).

Continual improvents to the M-82 engine at Factory № 19 (Perm) led to yet another new and more powerful version. The M-82FN was cleared for mass production early in 1943, and by March examples of a new La-5 variant were being tested at Gor'ki. The new aircraft was designated "La-5FN", again referencing the engine type, and making use of the Type 39 airframe. Early examples of the La-5FN (or, *Type 39 M-82FN*) were literally La-F models with the new -FN motor. These aircraft featured a slightly rounded aft end cowling, as with previous models, but with revised latches and a lengthened intake scoop.

However, there were ambitious plans afoot to apply many design improvements as suggested by NII VVS, LII and indeed factory testing. A list of these improvements would be formidable, but to be fair a great number of these were very specific detail modifications. The greatest suggested change was put forward by the NKAP strongly, this the proposal to manufacture the main wing spars out of duralumin. The situation *vis a vis* strategic materials had eased to the point where dural components were being applied to many new designs, and the use of spars of this type would represent a useful weight savings.

Ultimately, this major change to La-5 production proved to be too ambitious. The staff at Factory № 21 were struggling with many contemporary issues, and production examples were routinely failing to meet the agreed quality control standards. The introduction of dural spars at this time was simply impossible. Grudgingly, the government instructed Gor'ki to carry on with the new La-5FN model with the current wood-plastic spars.

Even so, some of the proposed detail modifications were introduced on the series manufactured -FN versions, the La-5FN *massovii*. The most dramatic change was a new cowling unit with a squarish, cylindrical shape, and retaining the lengthened intake along the upper surface. The new cowling had a greatly revised latching mechanism, with the fasteners placed at the bottom of the panels which folded upwards, being hinged in the middle. There were three vents on the stainless steel exhaust plate now, not two, and these were positioned aft. Most notably, thick dural sheet was added aft of the stainless steel plate for additional heat protection (from the engine exhaust), and along the wing roots to reduce surface wear from pilot entry and crew refuelling.

Ironically, the addition of external sheet to the airframe was an insufficient modification in the eyes of the Gor'ki staff to warrant a new type designation. The airframe was still a Type 39, and as seen previously, any changes to the engine and cowling simply did not register with those responsible for nomenclature at the factory. As with the earlier M-82F models, the Lavochkin OKB staff designed an "FN" badge to be placed on the cowling, identifying the engine. Both the early round "FN" and current "F" badges were increasingly applied not only to the cowl, but also on the tip of the rudder. Most La-5FN *massovii* models received a revised diamond shaped "FN" logo sometime thereafter.

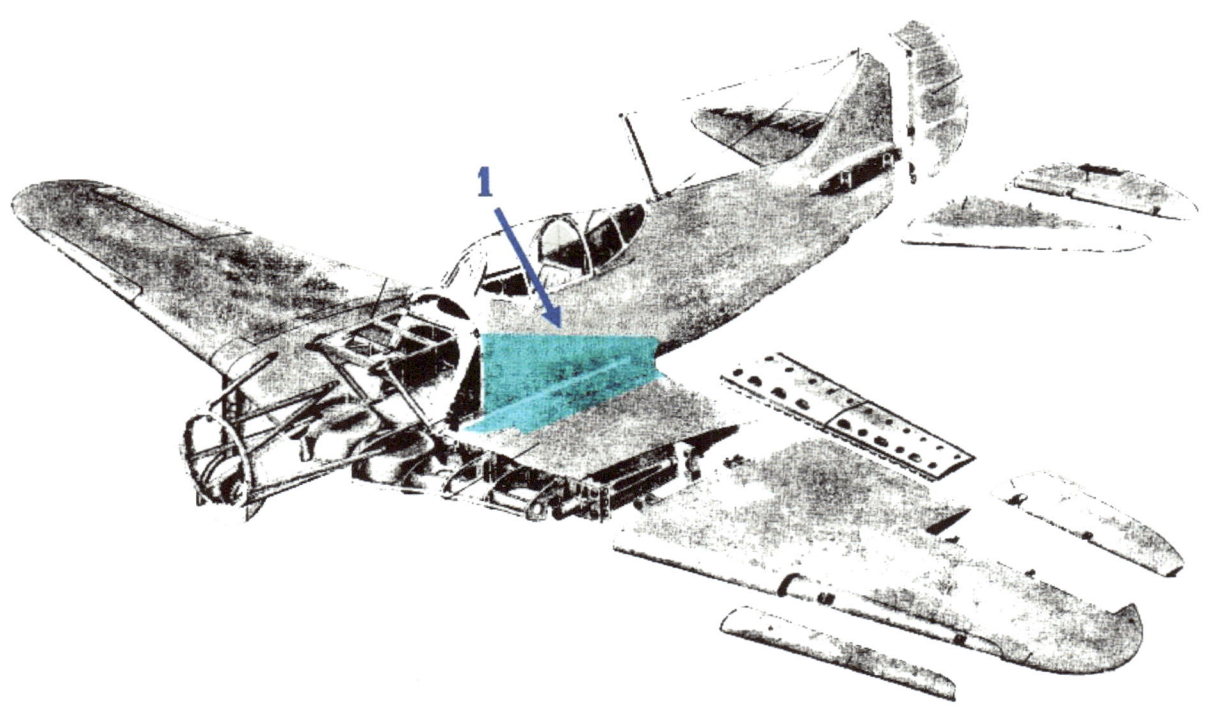

The Type 39 airframe for the La-5FN massovii featured only one major external change, these being three pieces of dural sheet (1.) placed on each side of the fuselage, and on the wing roots.

The Lavochkin early round "FN" badge [Left], and the later diamond style [Right].

By the end of 1943 the vast array of technical and manufacturing problems on the La-5 programme had been solved. Once again, therefore, the NKAP took up the idea to install metal wing spars on the -FN model, and indeed with such urgency that they even authorised delays in production should these arise in the process of re-tooling. By March 1944 series examples of La-5FNs with metal spars were at last leaving the production lines at Gor'ki, and by the summer also at Moscow and Ulan-Ude.

Naturally, the staff at Factory № 21 recognised these structural changes as a new airframe type, and assigned the designation "Type 41" to the metal spar La-5FNs; there was no *offical* (e.g. from Moscow) change in nomenclature.

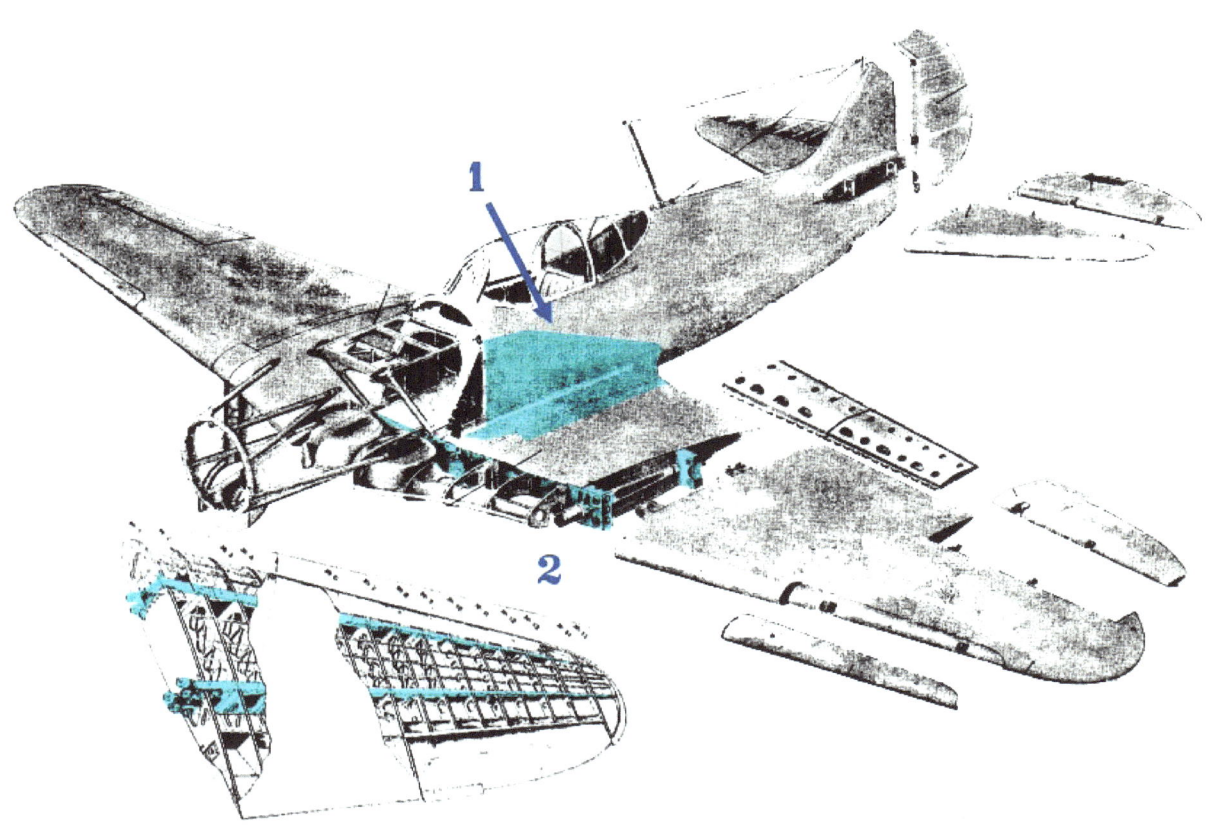

External changes to the Type 41 (1.) were mainly a minor re-shaping of the fuselage exhaust sheeting. The main modification (2.) consisted of dural main wing spars.

The final development in the La-5 programme at Gor'ki was the manufacture of a two-seat training version of the aircraft. This new airframe was christened the "Type 43" at the factory, and the La-5UTI everywhere else. Early examples were completed with the M-82F engine, and it was in this form that the NII VVS tested the prototype aircraft. Series manufacture was authorised by the government, this to be undertaken at Factory № 167 (Penza) by assembling components shipped from Gor'ki, and the intended engine was to have been the M-82FN.

In the event, series production of the UTI was not successful. The Factory № 167 staff were not experienced with the La-5's construction methods, and, as could be foreseen, the finished examples were over-weight and featured a c.g. which was too far aft, resulting in serious directional instability. Production of the La-5UTI was terminated after some 30 examples had been built.

However, the concept of a two-set UTI La-5 was regarded as sound by many within the VVS. As a result, a fair number of custom La-5UTI conversions were completed by units in the field, and also in small batches by various PARMs. As with two-seat Il-2 field conversions, some of these local examples were so good that they were examined under State Trials conditions by the NII VVS.

Ultimately, by 1944, attention was switching to the new La-7 programme, and plans were already afoot to create a UTI version of this fighter. As a result, interest in the UTI La-5 waned, and no further development was undertaken.

The La-5 Family in Scale Line Drawings

The line drawings presented herein are entirely new, never before published. These represent the culmination of many years' labour, and are based where possible on direct measurements taken from pieces of existing examples. These drawings build on the excellent and popular work published by Voronin and Rodinov, these based on the NKAP LaGG-3 and La-5FN Maintenance Manuals. A re-evaluation of the data in these documents, in addition to measurements taken from a recently discovered La-5 cockpit section, ailerons, wing spar and other parts has provided new insight into the original shapes and details of this iconic fighter aircraft.

Production of the La-5 began at Factory № 21 in Gor'ki (now Nizhniy Novgorod). The earliest models were, indeed, very little more than pre-production hybrids, and these were built in strictly limited numbers. Full-scale mass production began with what the local staff called the "Type 37" (referring to specific types of aircraft built at this plant was a habit which extended back to the I-16 programme, and even before), this with leading edge wing slats, a new windscreen, and other detail improvements. Later, the first La-5F models to appear were also known at Gor'ki as "Type 37s", simply sporting a new engine.

The "Type 39" introduced the cut-down rear fuselage and clear canopy aft section which was so iconic of the typical (*massovii*) La-5F and later La-5FN models. A last version, the Type 41, introduced weight savings via metal wing spars, and these were followed by the Type 43 two-seat training models. The next type assignment known to Factory 21 would be the "45", and that is the story-- to be told later-- of the La-7.

All of the primary scale line drawings in this volume are presented in 1:48 scale. In cases where scrap or detail views are rendered in another scale, these will be noted directly on the drawing.

As with all scale line drawings, it is often the case that certain details are deliberately omitted from oblique views where such items would be either difficult to render, or might be misleading in a flat projection. This is so, often, as a result of the curvature or shape of the structure, leading to problems of representing such detail in a two-dimensional plane. The small rivets present on underwing panels or cowling seams when viewed from a side projection are examples of this kind of problem, and in these drawings have been omitted in those views. *As a result, readers are advised to consult the most perpendicular line drawing available for the definitive level of detail over any given area of the aircraft.*

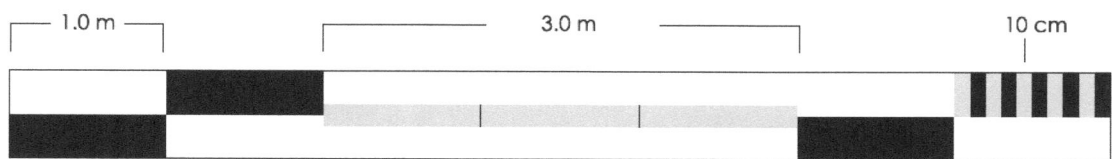

The Gu-82 Prototype

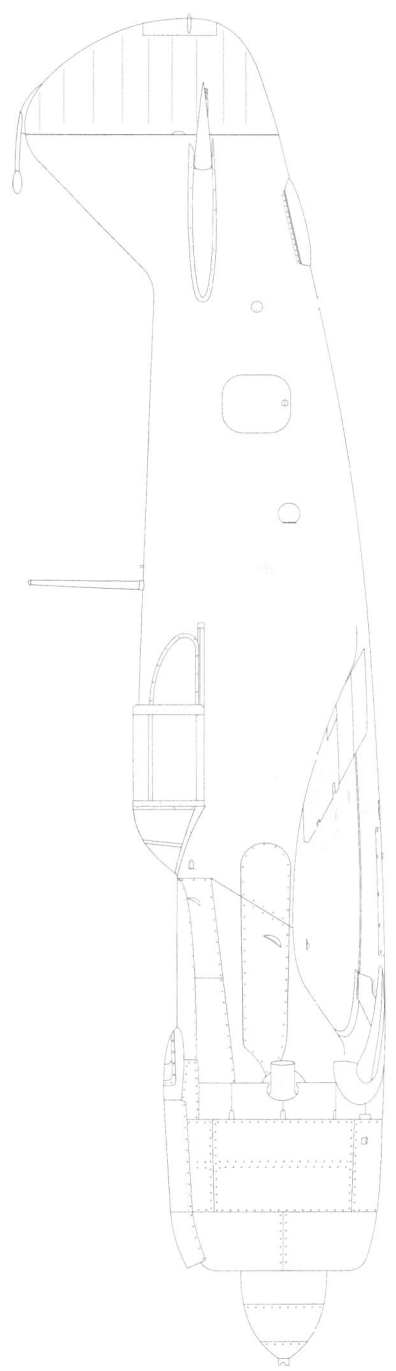

It would perhaps be difficult to find a more frequently misidentified aircraft in published photographs than Gudkov's Gu-82 prototype. Invariably, images of either the Gor'ki built LaGG-3 № 1 or № 2 prototypes are labelled as the "Gu-82", of course, this is incorrect. In fact, so far as the author is aware, there have not as yet materialised *any* photographs of the actual Gudkov M-82 prototype. We do have a number of written descriptions of the machine, of course, and it is upon that data that this reconstructive line drawing is based.

Having said all that, the Gu-82 would surely have looked very much like this drawing. A pre-production LaGG-3 airframe was used in the Factory № 301 workshop to build the prototype, and Gudkov's own technical description of his method for blending the power-plant unit (from an Su-2, in fact) into the fuselage fits the details in view here. Additionally, the drawing shows the retention of all possible LaGG-3 features on the aircraft, as befitting the very short development schedule of the Gu-82.

LaGG-3 M-82 №1

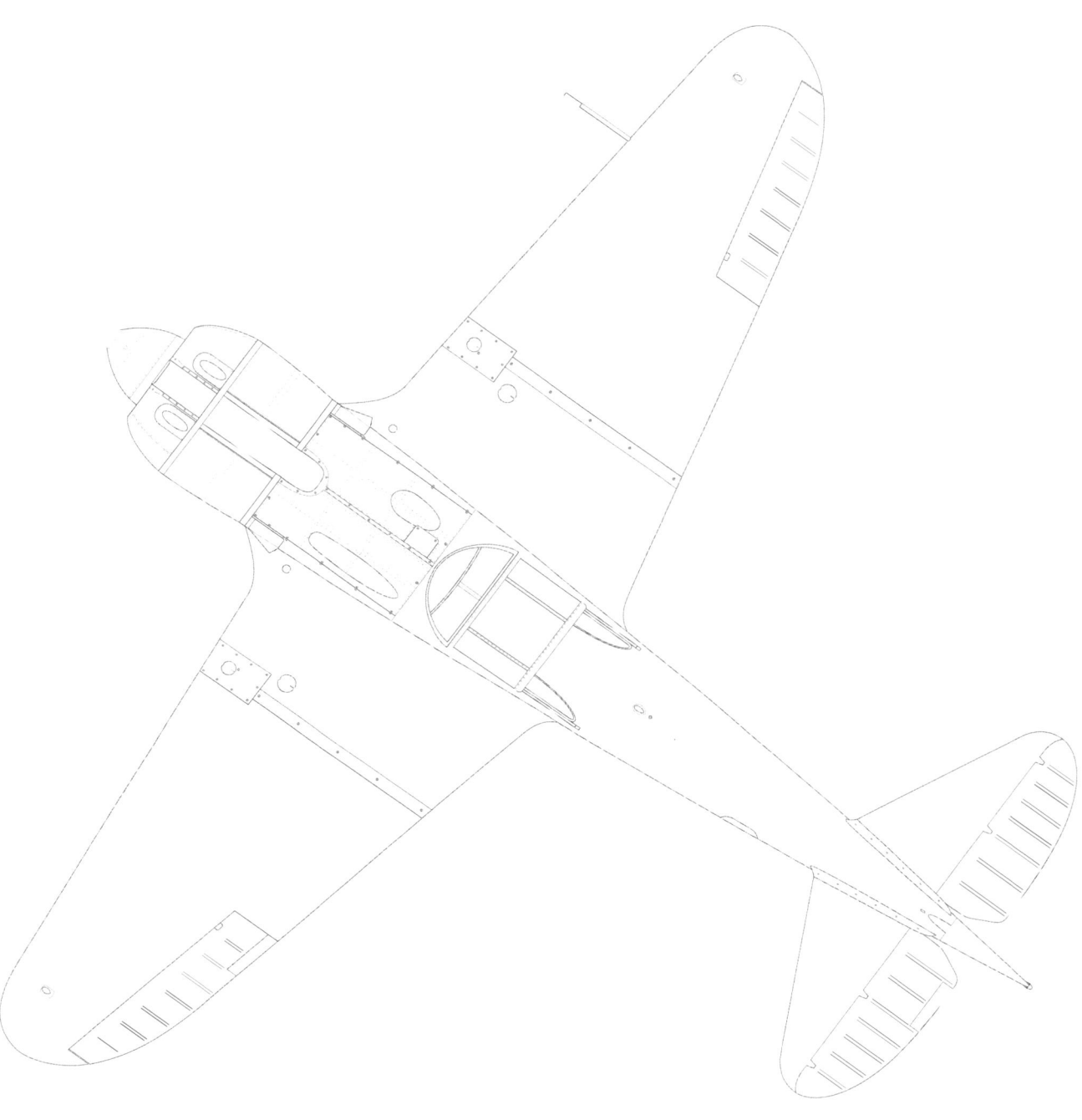

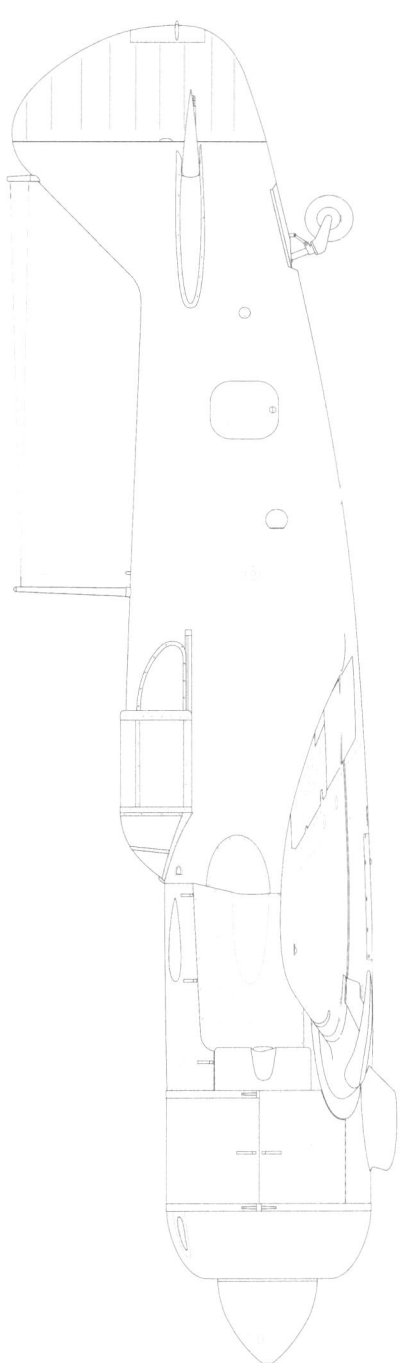

The first Gor'ki built LaGG-3 M-82 prototype was completed using a contemporary massovii LaGG airframe (Type 31), likely from Series 15 or 16 (or thereabouts). The cowling was especially curious in that it featured a squarish, cylindrical form, not unlike that of the later La-5FN. The forward cowl ring was slightly enlarged compared to the series La-5 family, but the cowl panels hinged in way common to later production types.

The upper cowl cover was custom made for the aircraft, as was the stainless steel plate mounted aft of the exhaust. The original LaGG-3 round dural plate was retained, however, and no significant modifications were undertaken on the airframe, itself.

The oil cooler was an item of special note. Chief Engineer Slepnev had designed a custom unit of minimal drag and aerodynamic shape, this based upon some computational data from Factory № 19 regarding M-82 cooling. Alas, the factory data proved to be faulty, and the № 1's oil cooler to be inadequate for the job.

LaGG-3 M-82 № 2

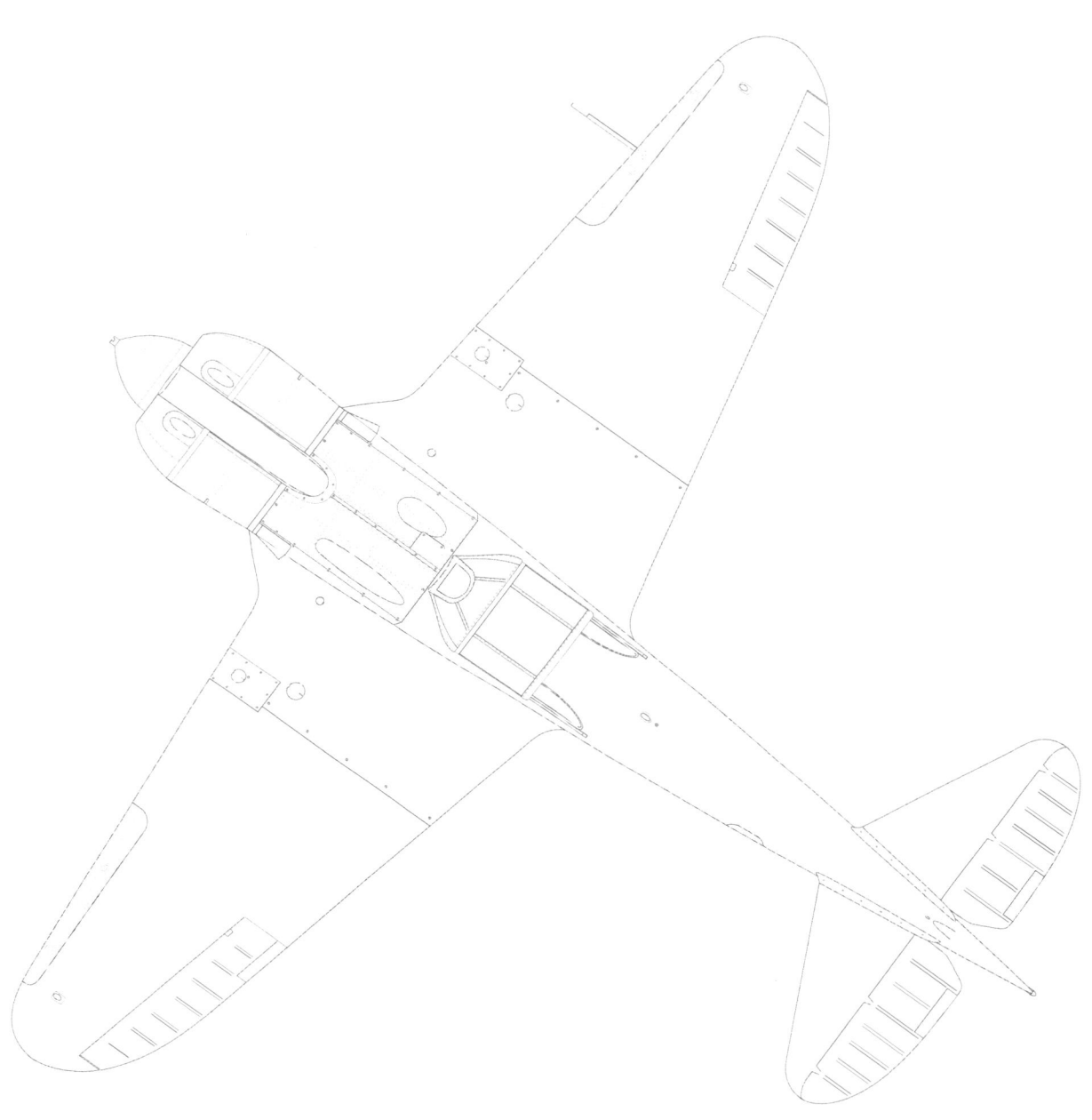

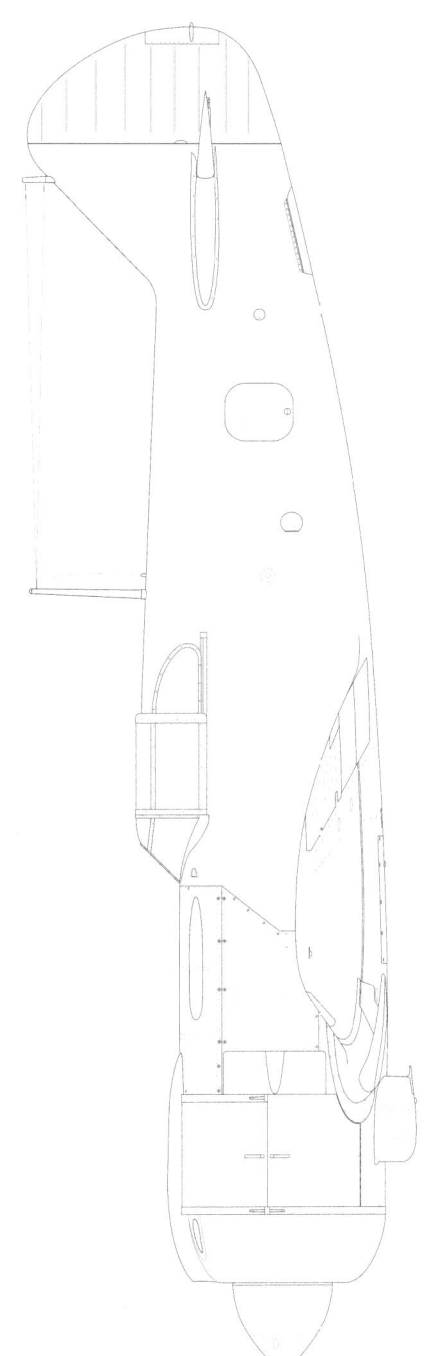

The second Gor'ki built LaGG-3 M-82 prototype was completed using a contemporary *massovii* LaGG airframe (Type 31), but with aerodynamic refinements essentially equal to the Type 37 standard. Leading edge wing slats were installed, as was the Type 37's flat windscreen and flush retractable tail wheel.

The hinged cowl access doors featured a close-fitting aft edge which imparted the classic "onion" shape to the La-5's planform view. In fact, virtually all of the cowling was identical to the *massovii* La-5 save for the shape of the stainless steel exhaust plate, and the full-length intake scoop which was similar to that used on the later La-5FN.

A larger oil cooler was installed on the № 2, and this would become the standard unit for the remainder of the La-5 family.

LaG-5 and LaGG-5
Factory № 21 (Gor'ki)

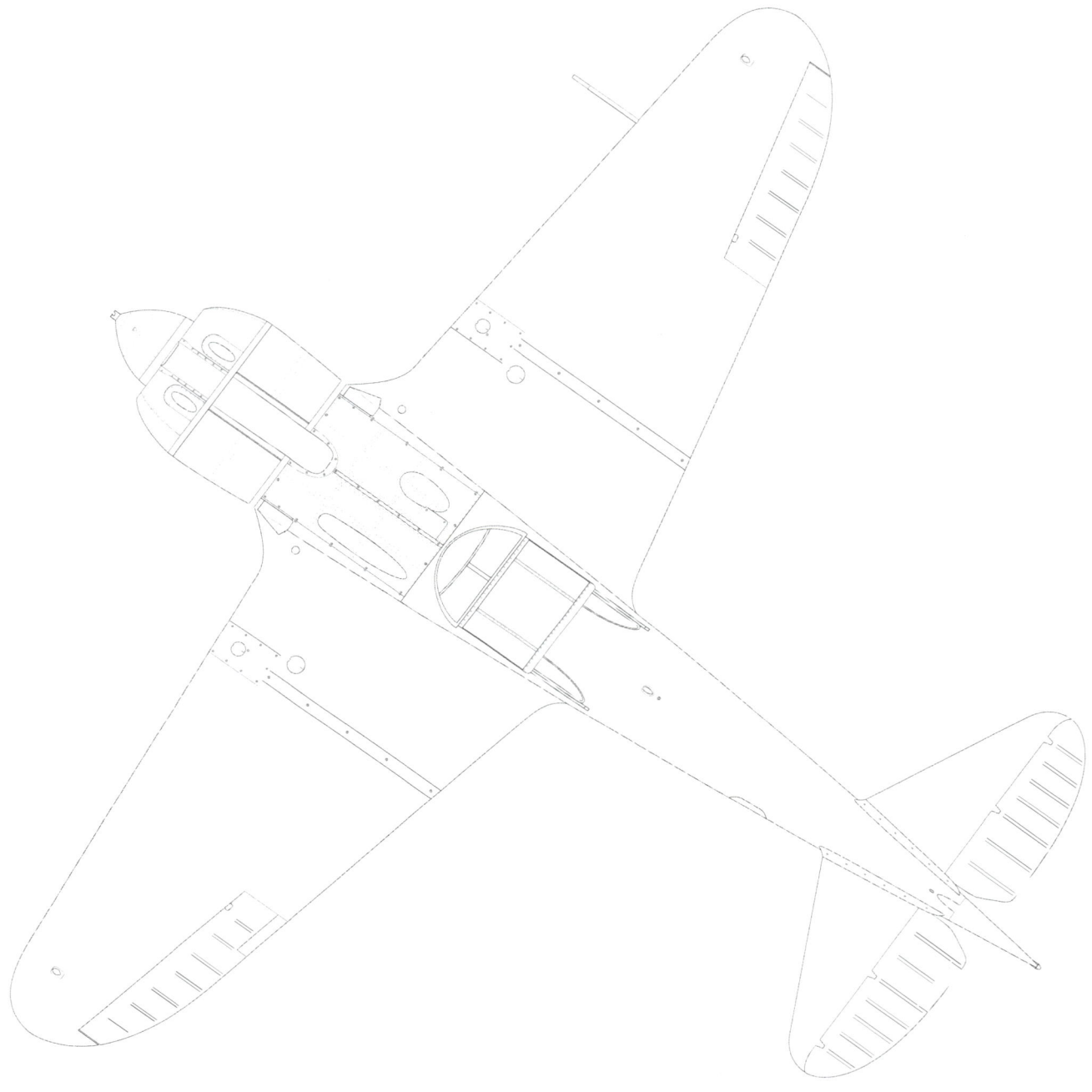

New or notable features in view:
- No leading edge wing slats
- Cockpit adjustable aileron trim tab, port only
- No wing mounted landing light
- LaGG style rounded windscreen

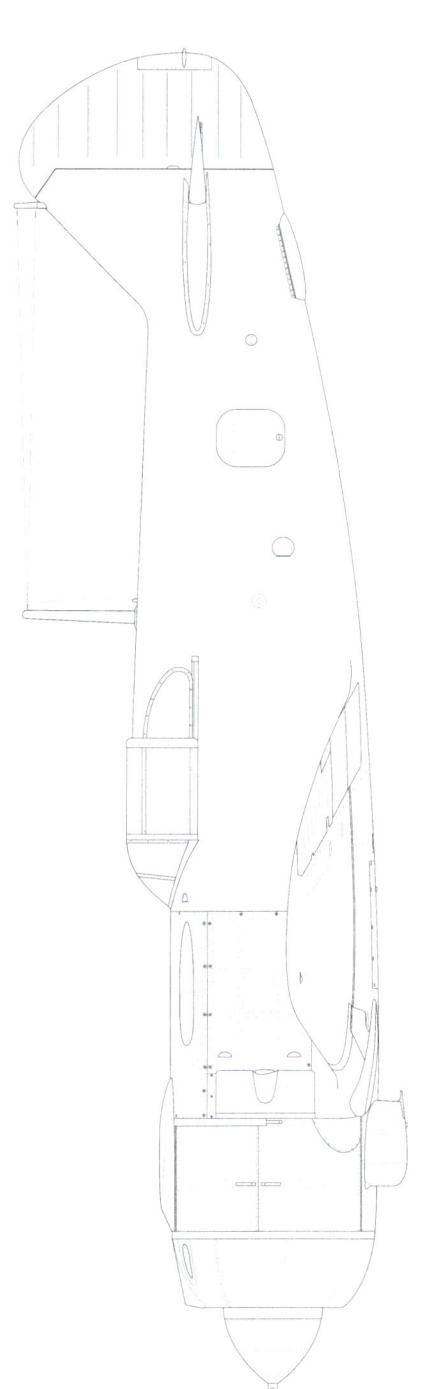

Port view LaGG-5 example built at Factory № 21 (Gor'ki)

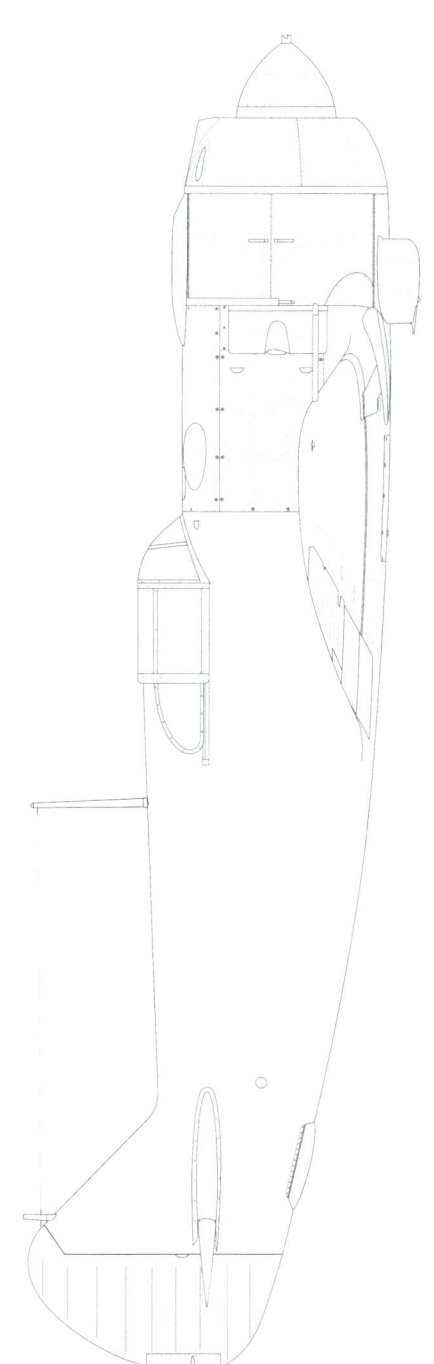

Starboard view LaGG-5 example built at Factory № 21 (Gor'ki)

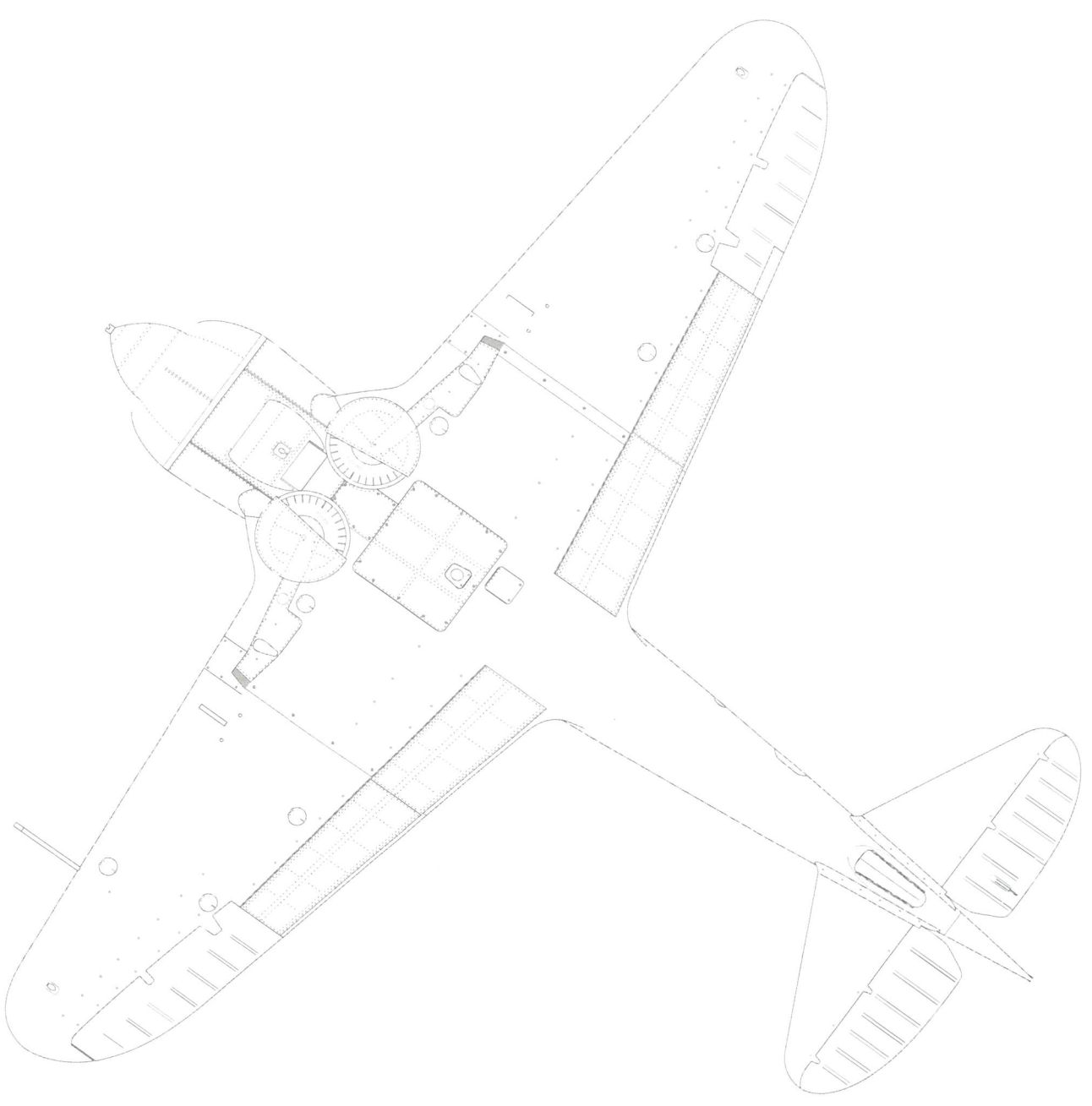

New or notable features in view:
- *No leading edge wing slats*
- *Cockpit adjustable aileron trim tab, port only*
- *No wing mounted landing light*
- *29 small air bleed holes as per LaGG-3*
- *Uncovered bomb rack attachment fitting slots*

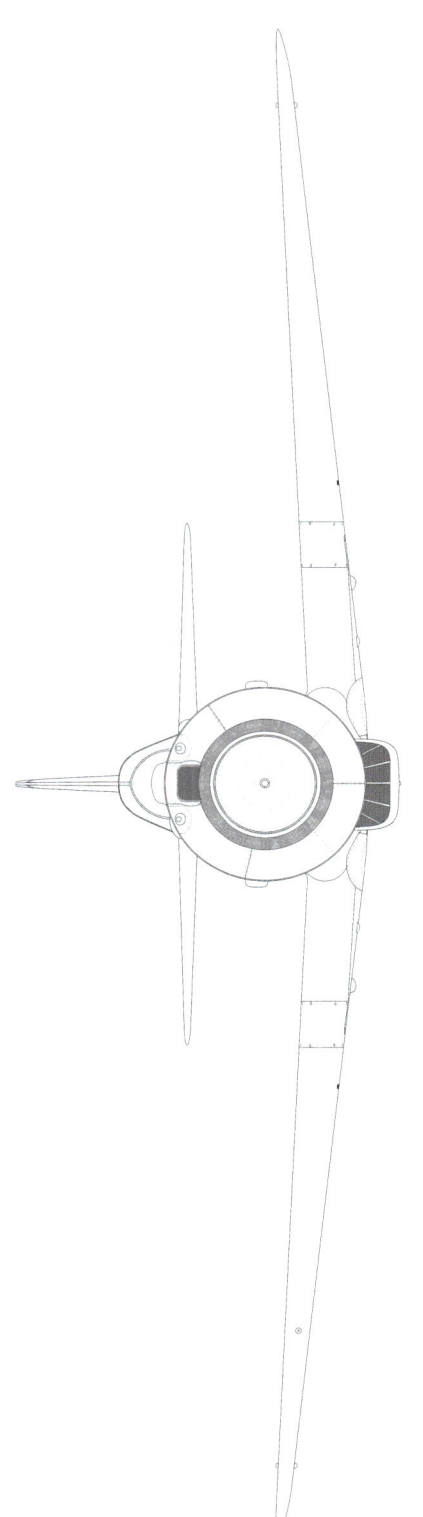

Front view of a typical LaG-5 or LaGG-5 hybrid. The LaGG airframe features are very apparent.

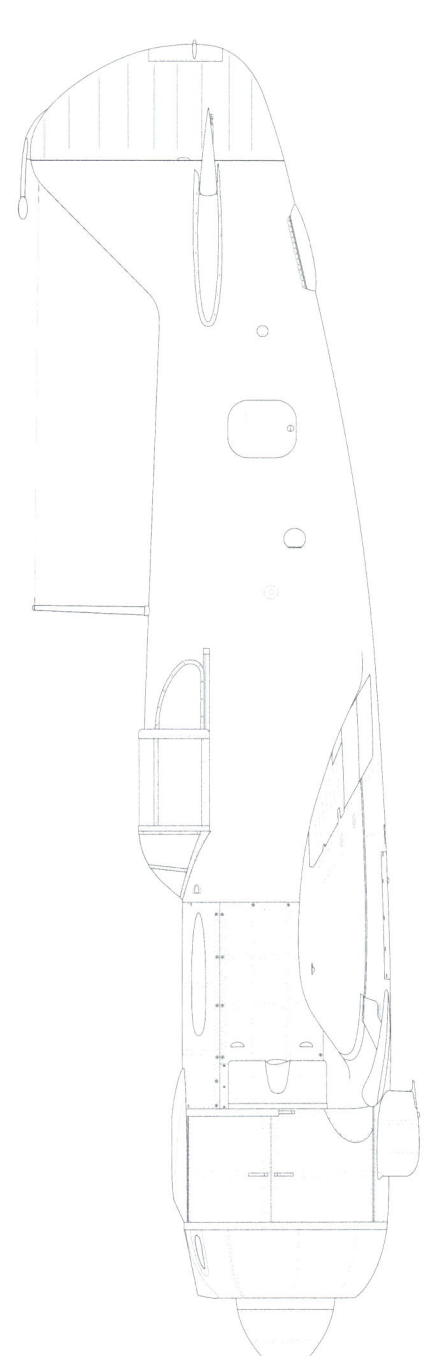

LaG-5 example built at Factory № 31 (Tbilisi)

La-5 *massovii* (Type 37)
Factory № 21 (Gor'ki)

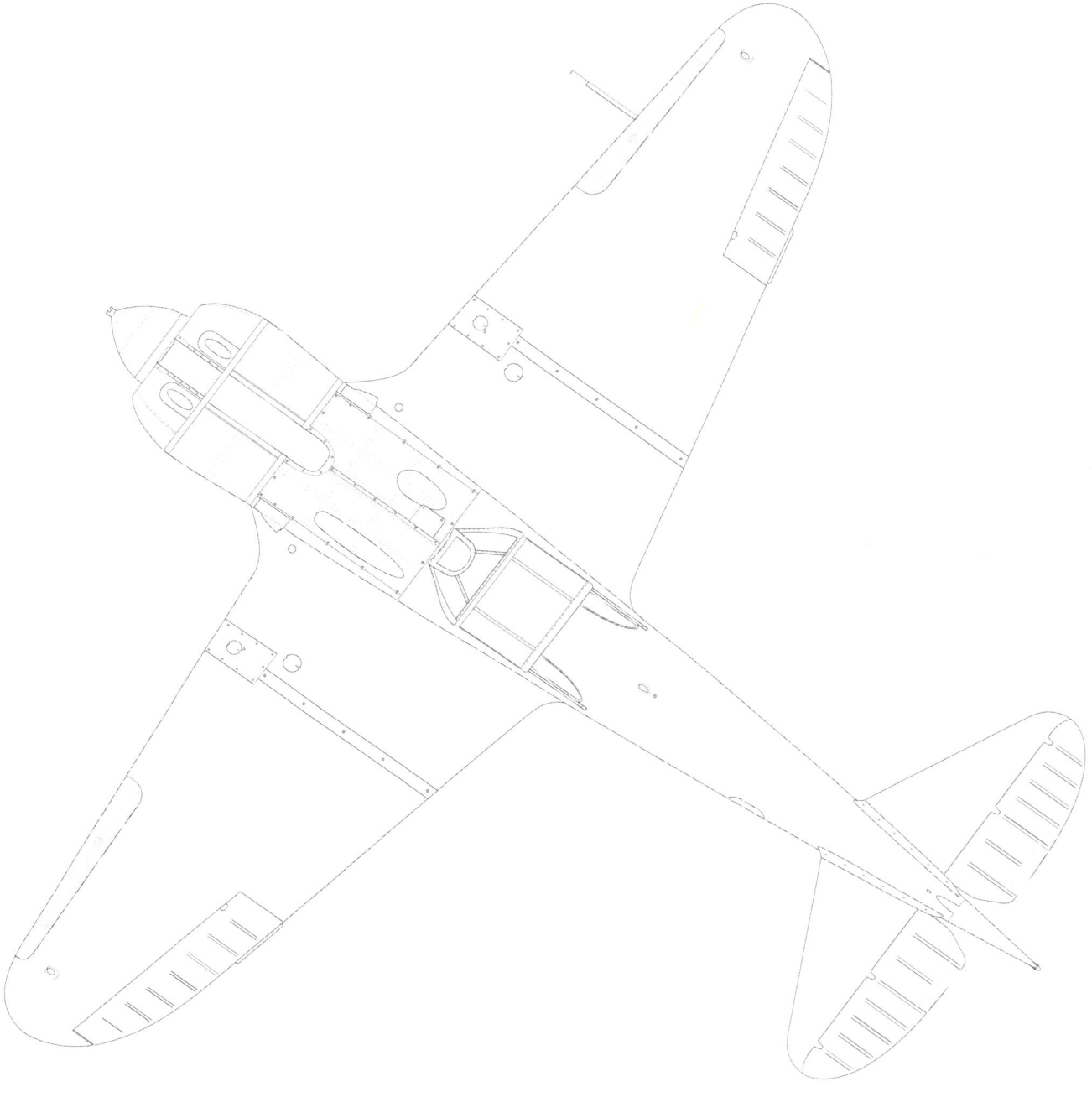

New or notable features in view:
- Leading edge wing slats
- Ground adjustable aileron trim tabs
- Revised radio mast, being thicker and slightly shorter

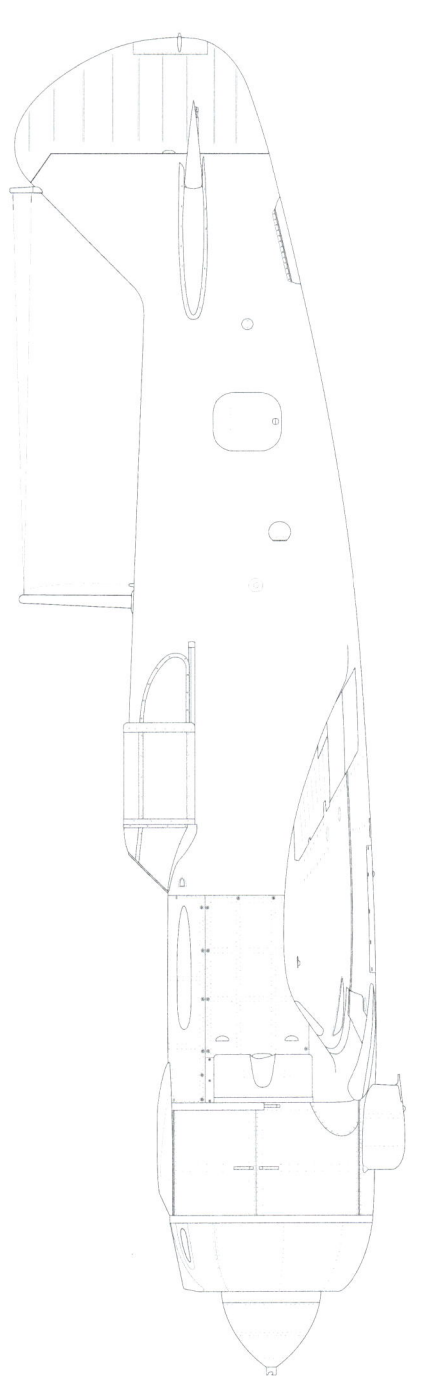

Port view La-5 (Type 37) *massovii* from Factory № 21 (Gor'ki)

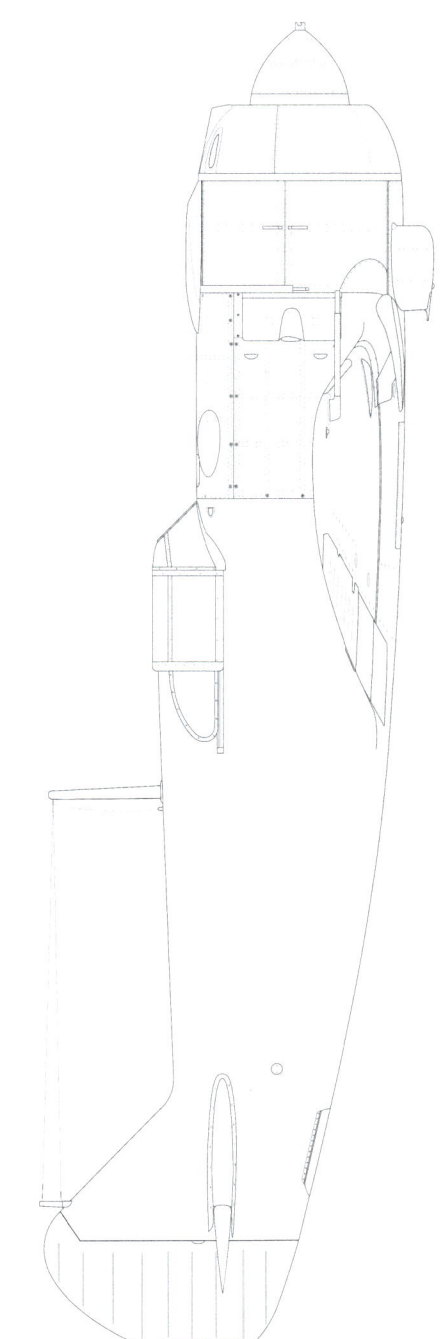

Starboard view La-5 (Type 37) *massovii* from Factory № 21 (Gor'ki)

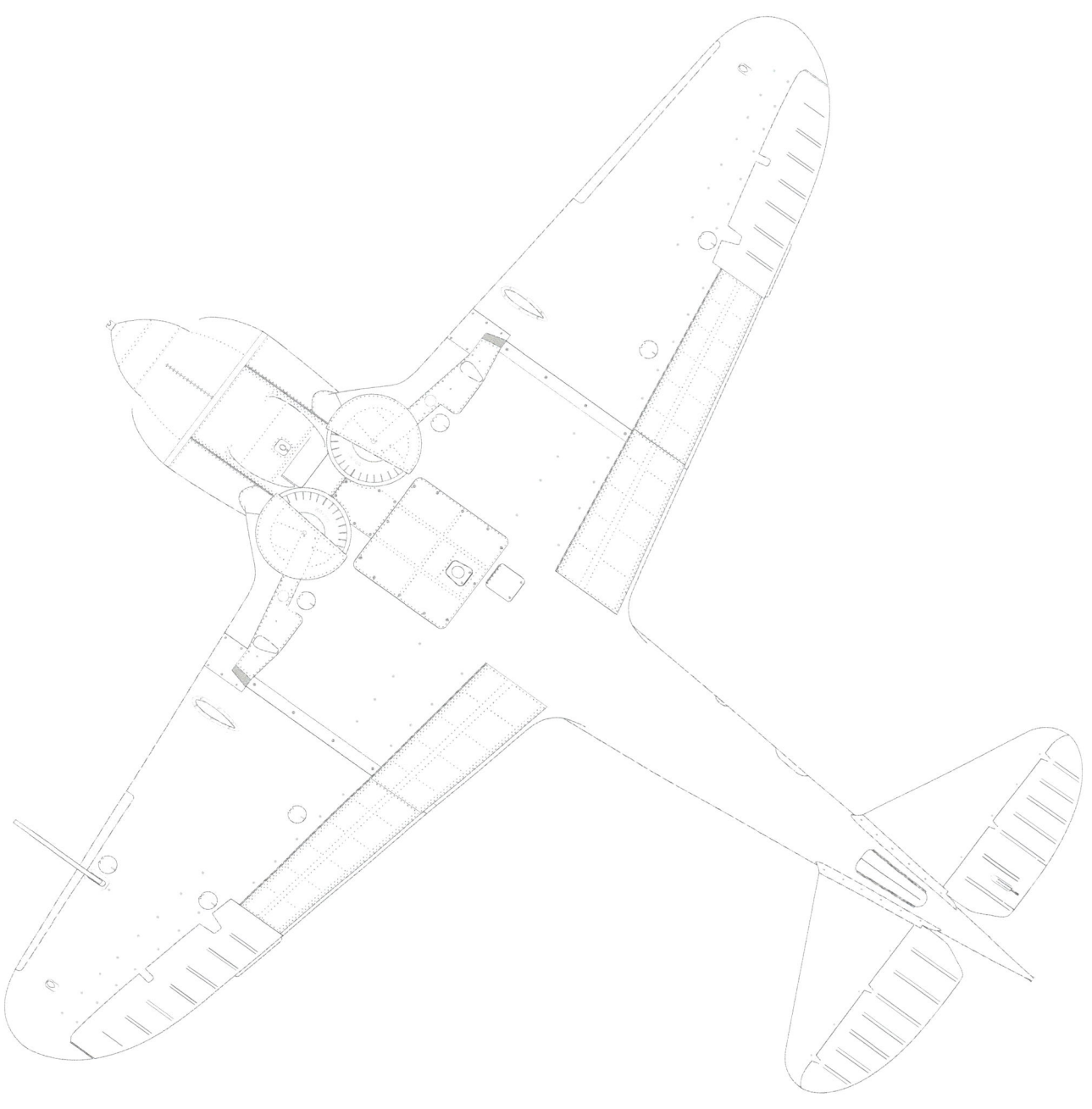

New or notable features in view:
- *Leading edge wing slats*
- *Ground adjustable aileron trim tabs*
- *Round central bulges on landing gear covers*
- *Pitot mounted below and aft of leading edge*
- *28 small air bleed holes (hole near pitot omitted)*
- *Small fairings over bomb rack attachment fitting holes*

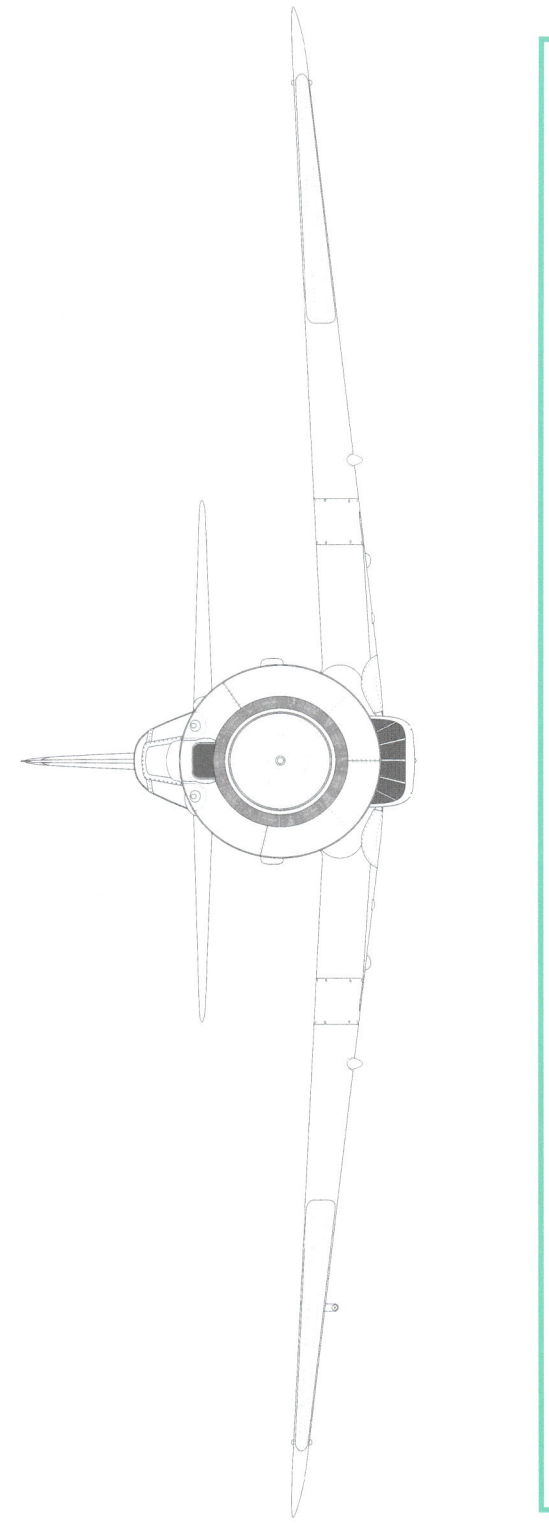

Front view La-5 (Type 37) *massovii* from Factory № 21 (Gor'ki)

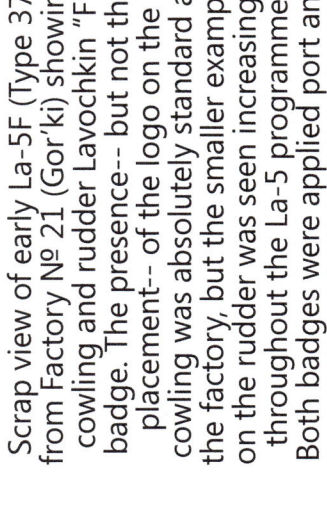

Scrap view of early La-5F (Type 37) from Factory № 21 (Gor'ki) showing cowling and rudder Lavochkin "F" badge. The presence– but not the placement– of the logo on the cowling was absolutely standard at the factory, but the smaller example on the rudder was seen increasingly throughout the La-5 programme. Both badges were applied port and starboard.

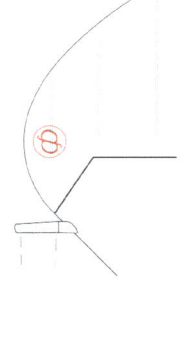

SCALE = 1:25

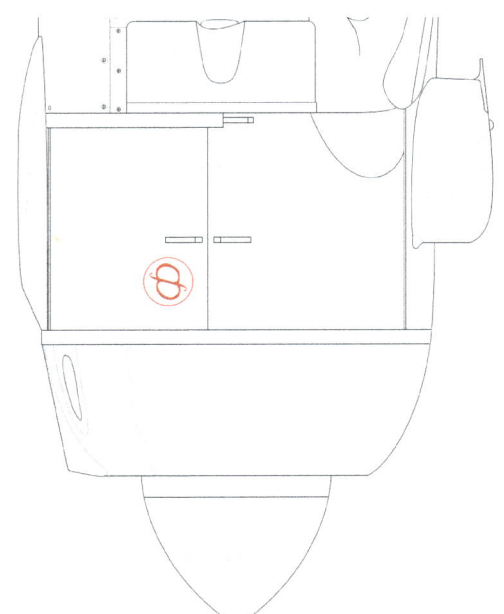

All Lavochkin fighters were built at the factory with internal mounting hardware for this bomb rack. However, as is shown clearly in the photographic record, it was rarely used. The rack was rated for a munition up to 50 kg (ergo, a FAB 50 or similar), but no image exists of a VVS Lavochkin mounting anything other than an AO-25M series smoke bomb (used for target marking), as seen here. Post war images of La-5FNs in Czech service show crews mounting both the Russian FAB 50 and German SC50 weapons.

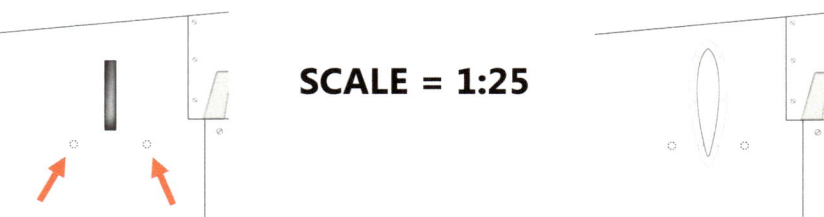

SCALE = 1:25

The LaGG-3 usually left the factory with the main mounting slot exposed [Left, above], which was cut through the entire wing skinning. However, the small holes at the aft end were cut only through the spruce sheet, but covered over by the resin-fabric exterior wrapping, and therefore cannot be seen. The La-5 [Right, above] introduced a fairing to cover this square slot which was screwed in place; not a mounting mechanism designed for repeated use. To fit the bomb rack, the rear holes would have to be cut through the resin-fabric covering, and subsequently when not in use one presumes that these would have to be filled with a plug (threaded or glued). These plugged holes are precisely what we *do not see* in the photographic record, as well as the rack itself.

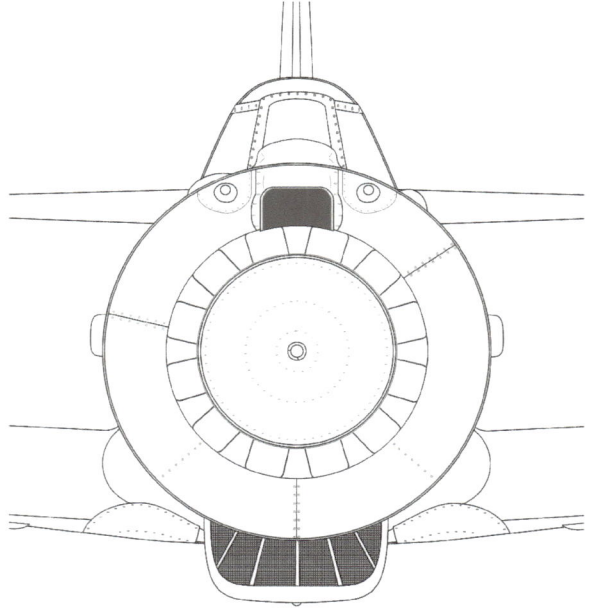

Scrap view of the louvres in the fully closed position, La-5 *massovii* (all other variants identical)

SCALE = 1:25

La-5F *massovii* (Type 39)
Factory № 21, 99, 381

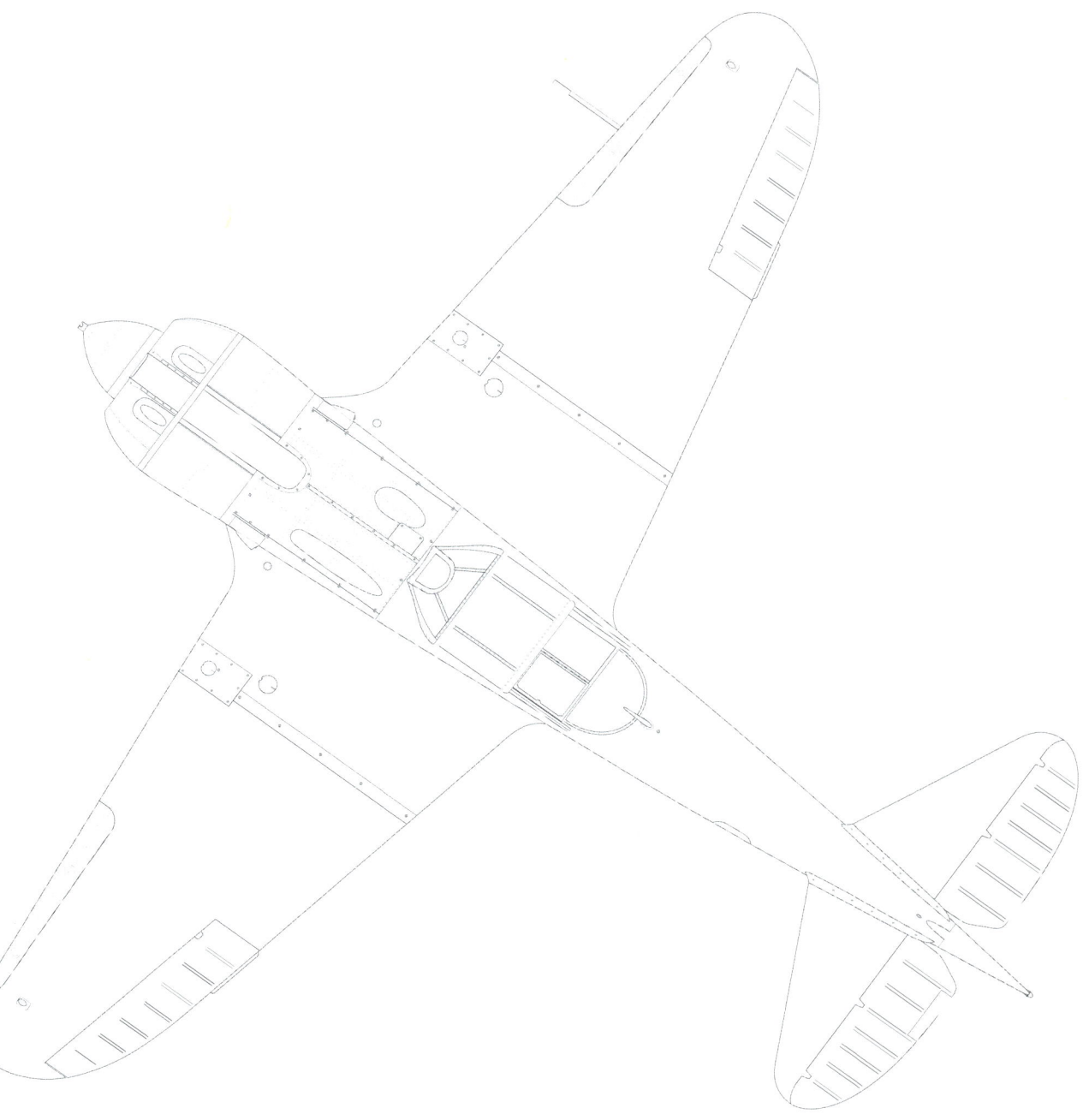

New or notable features in view:
- Cut-down rear fuselage with clear aft canopy section
- Hinged access door in rear canopy on port side
- Forward inclined radio mast

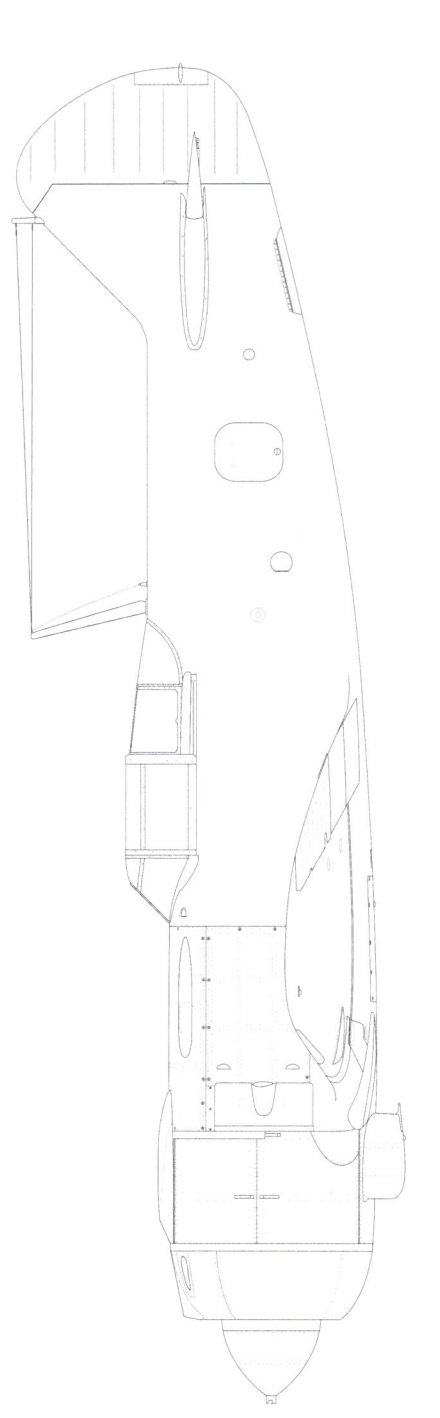

Port view La-5F (Type 39) *massovii*

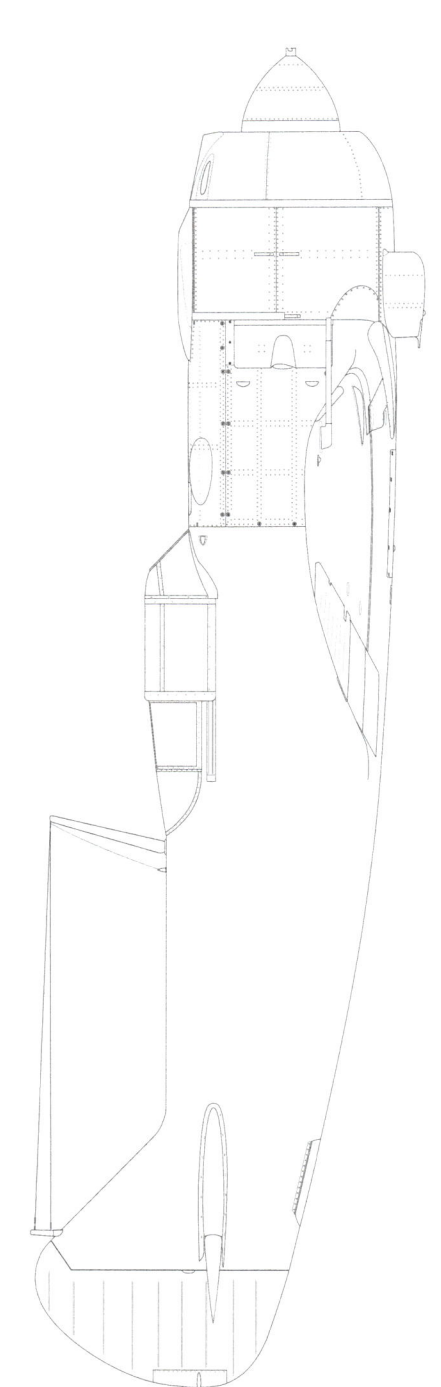

Starboard view La-5F (Type 39) *massovii*

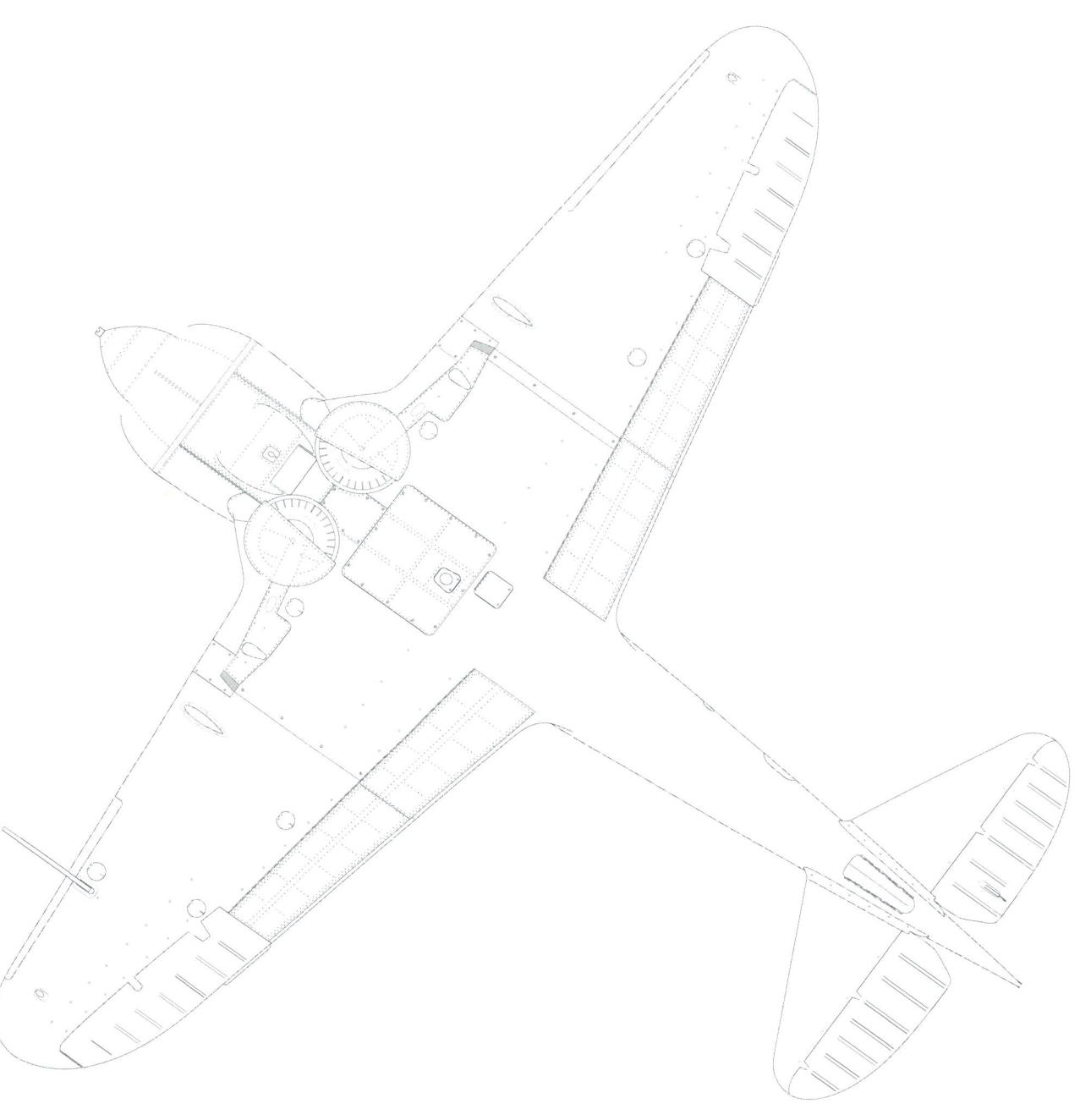

New or notable features in view:
- *Oval shaped central bulges on landing gear covers*

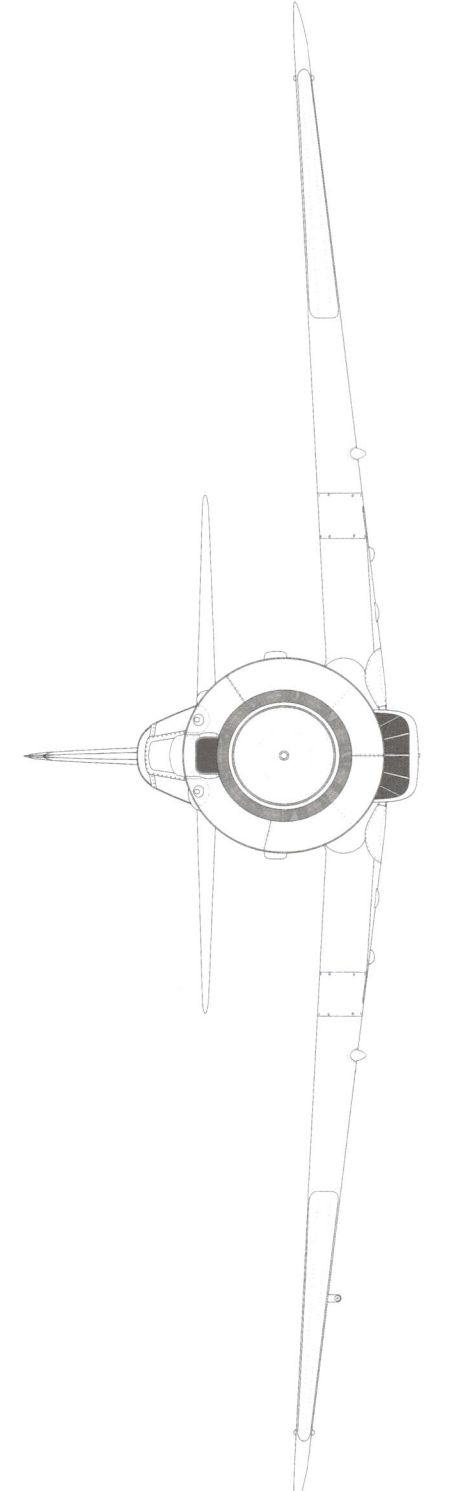

Front view La-5F (Type 39) *massovii*

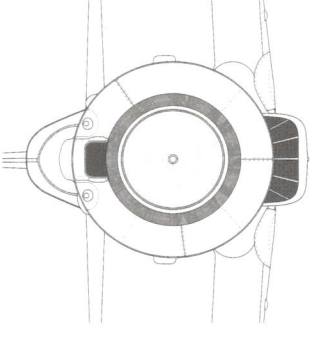

[Right] La-5F (Type 39) *massovii* with revised front cowl piece construction. One aircraft which clearly shows these features is known to have been built at Factory № 381 in Moscow, and no example known to have been manufactured at Gor'ki does so. It may well be the case that this detail does identify Moscow production La-5Fs and -FNs.

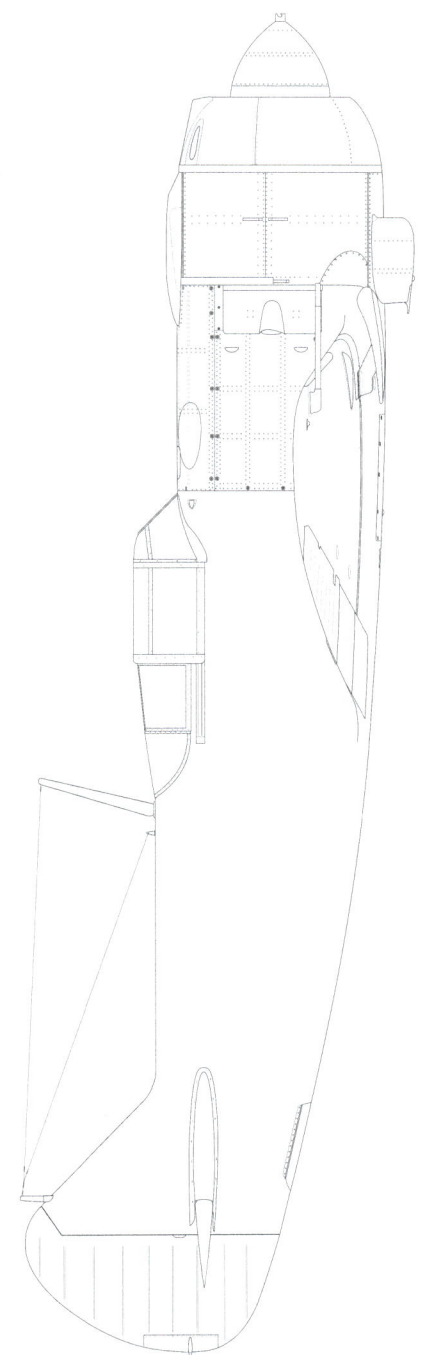

La-5F (Type 39) *massovii* with revised radio aerials. This style was increasing common on later models, and may have indicated a switch from the RSI-3 to the RSI-4 radio.

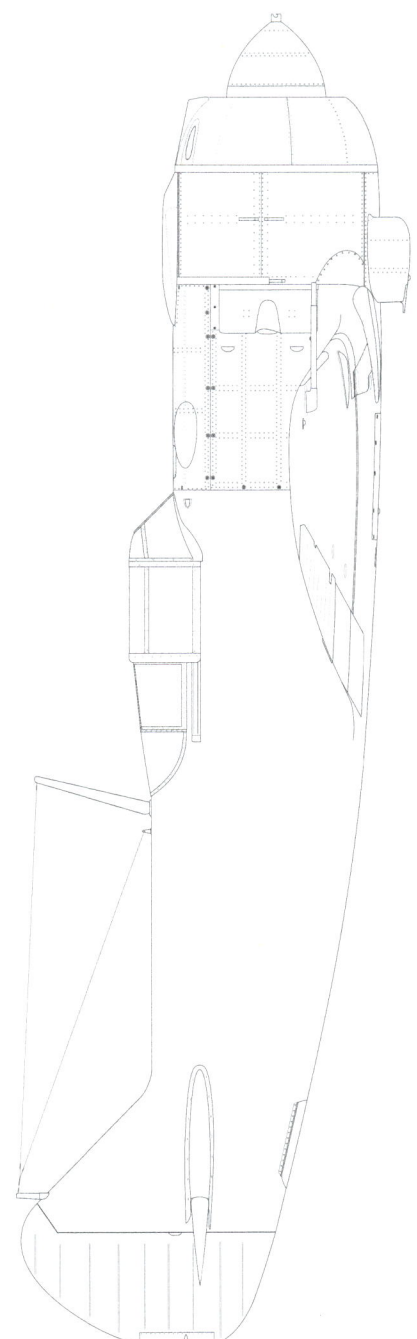

La-5F (Type 39) *massovii* with revised front cowl piece construction. The changes were seen only on the starboard side of the cowl; the port side was identical to the standard unit.

La-5FN 'early' (Type 39)
Factory № 21 (Gor'ki)

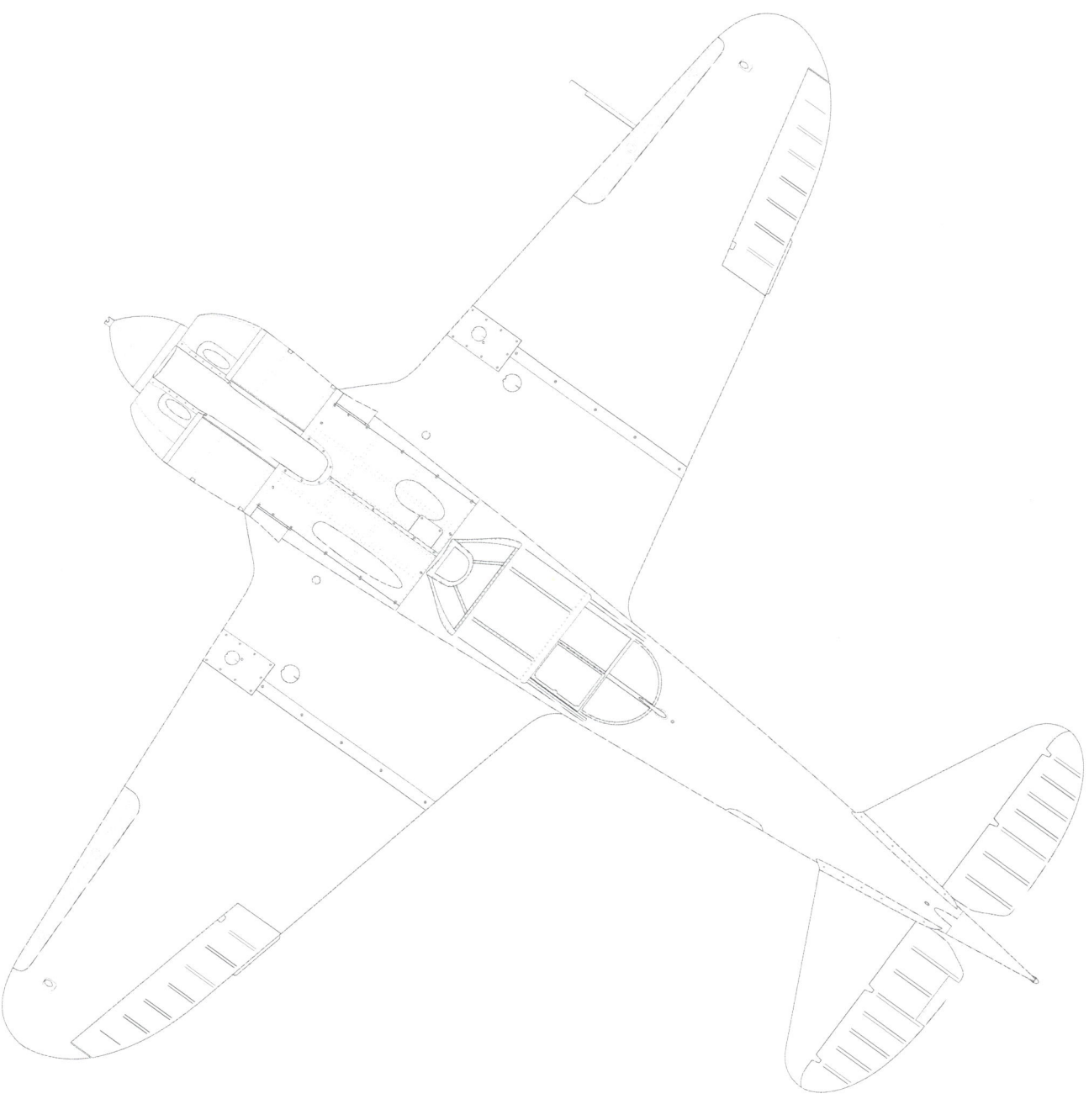

New or notable features in view:
- *Full-length intake trunk on top of cowling with revised width and details*

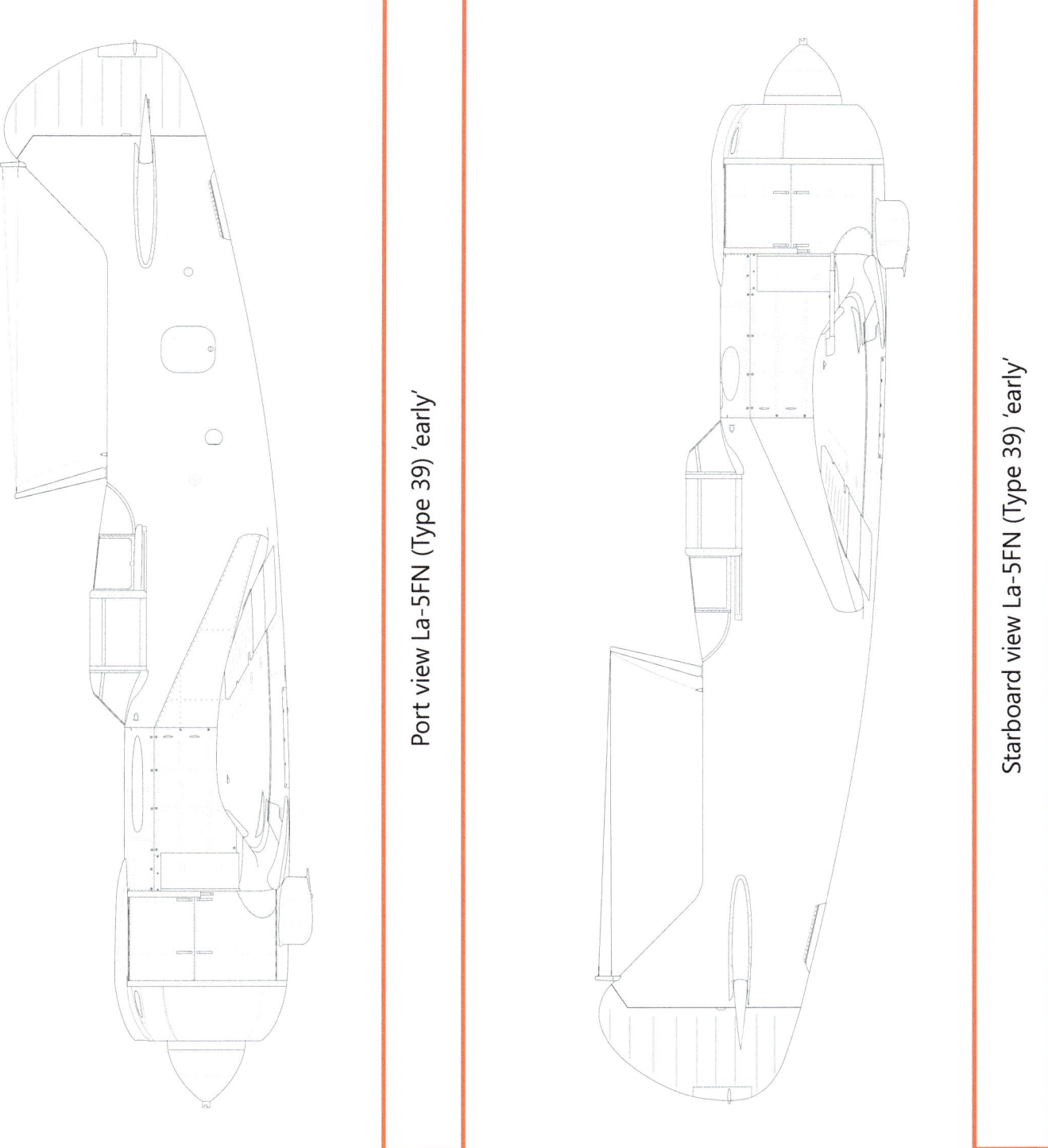

Port view La-5FN (Type 39) 'early'

Starboard view La-5FN (Type 39) 'early'

Underside view identical to La-5F massovii; see page 60
Front view identical to La-5FN massovii; see page 68

La-5FN *massovii* (Type 39)
Factory № 21, 99, 381

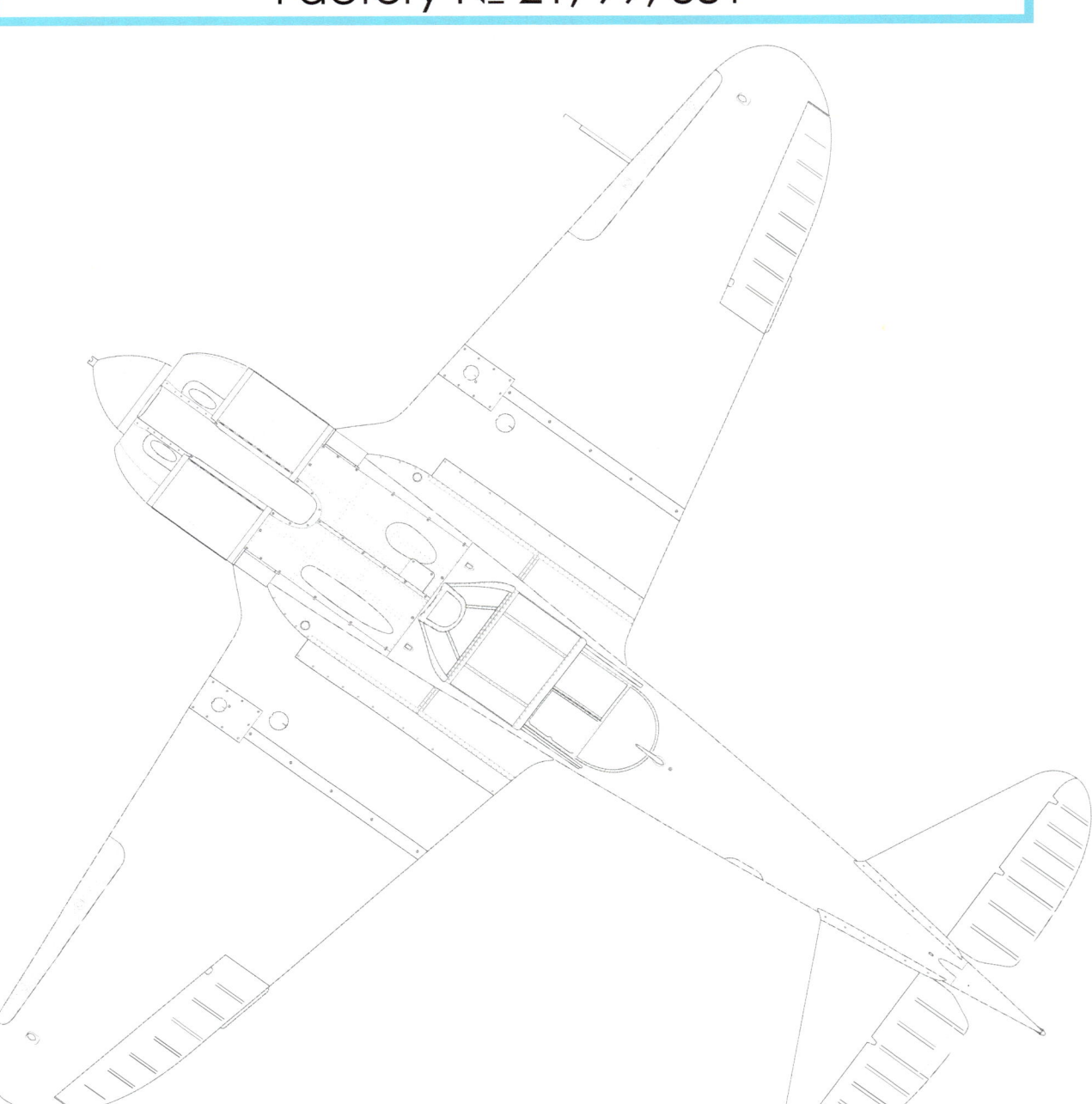

New or notable features in view:
- Cylindrical cowling with 'flat' sides
- Dural sheet pieces added to wing root and fuselage sides (8 in total)
- Small modification of wing root fillet shape aft edge where it meets the fuselage

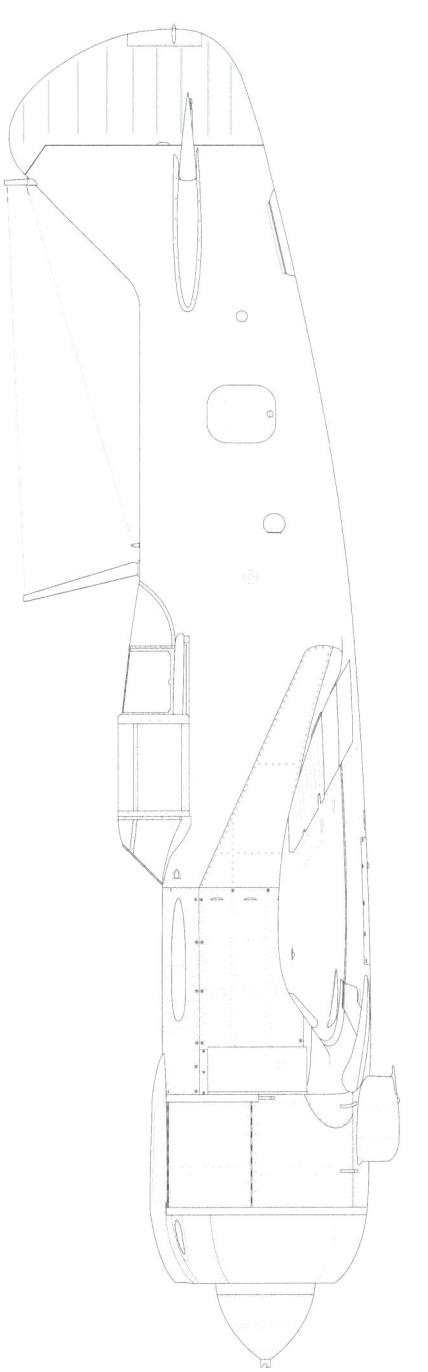

Port view La-5FN (Type 39) *massovii*

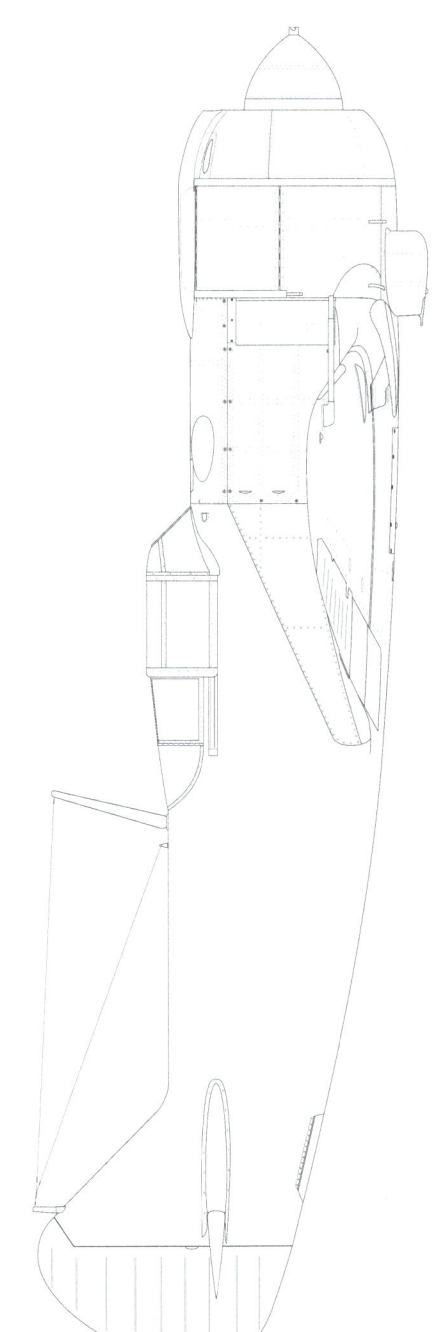

Starboard view La-5FN (Type 39) *massovii*

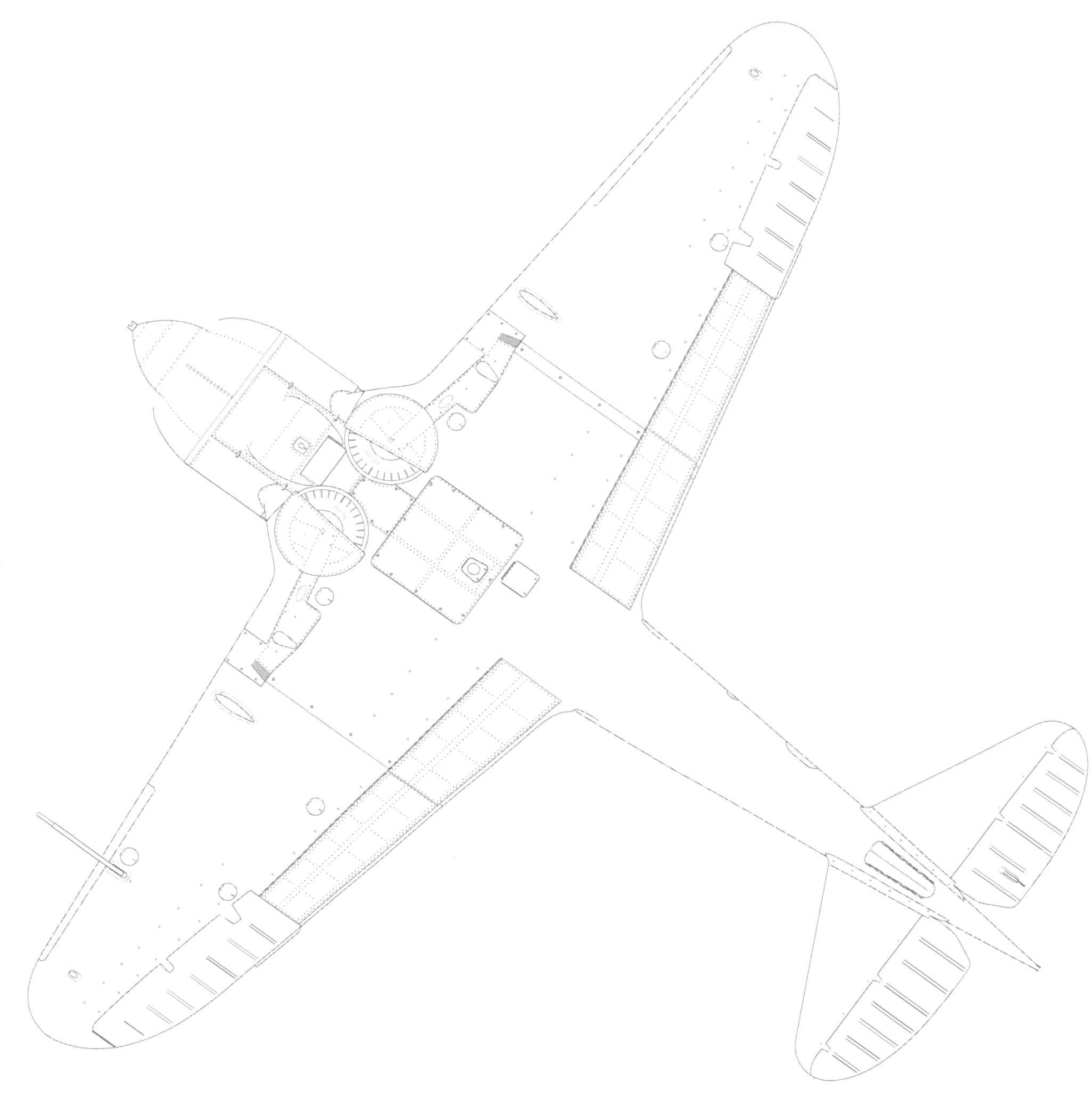

New or notable features in view:
- Cylindrical cowling with 'flat' sides
- Small modification of wing root fillet shape aft edge where it meets the fuselage

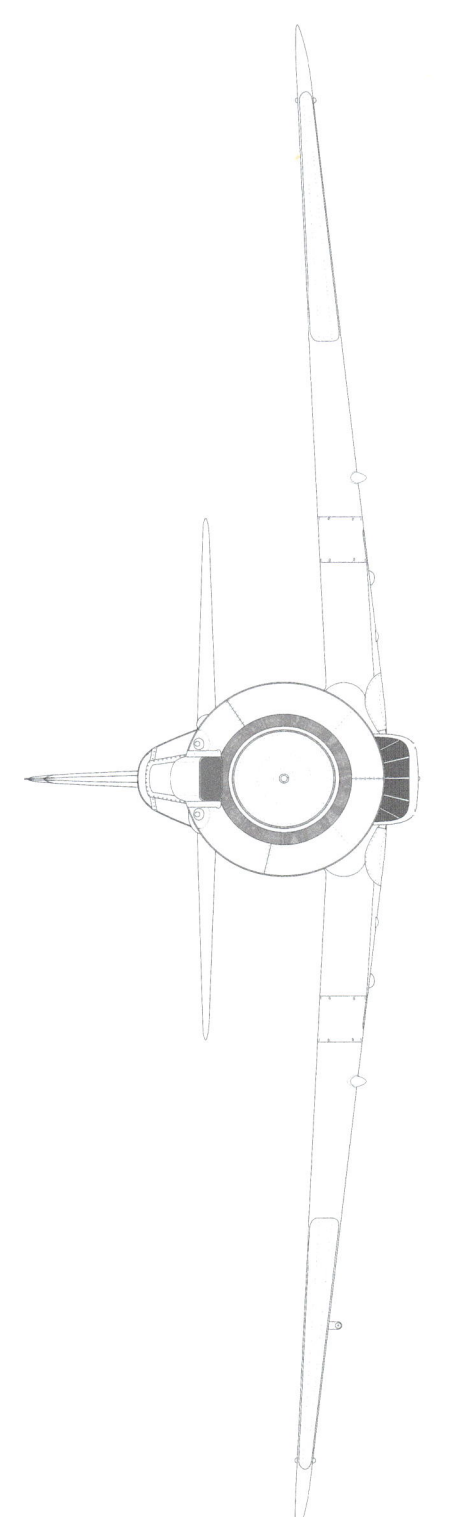

Front view La-5FN (Type 39) *massovii*

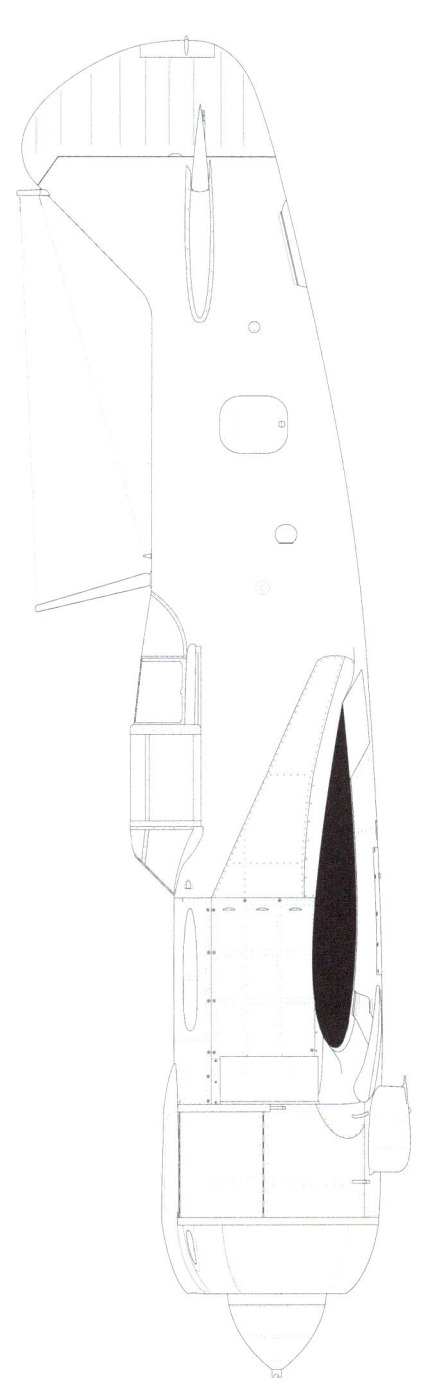

Port view La-5FN (Type 39) *massovii* with wing removed at the joint strap to show wing root details.

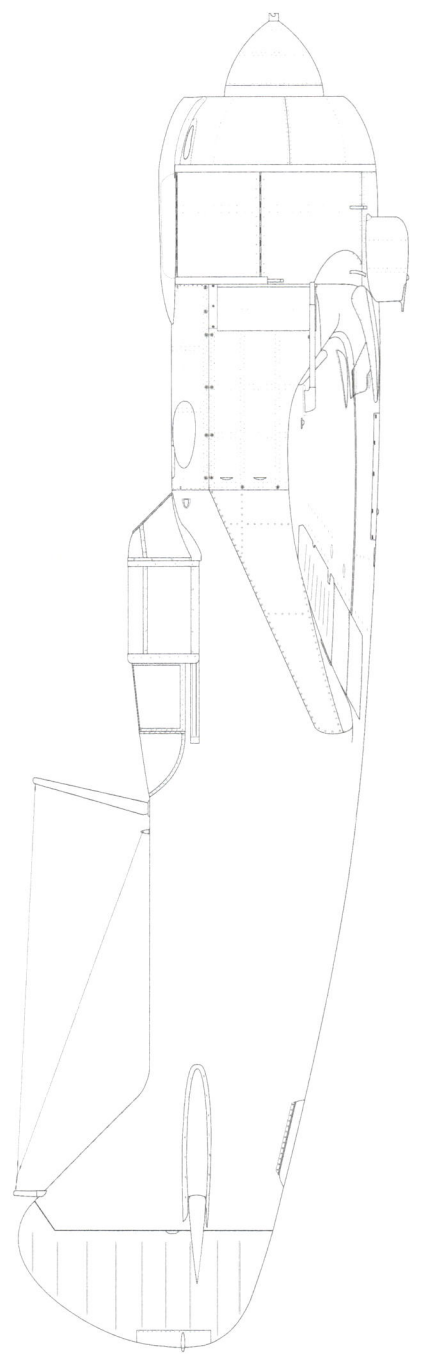

Port view La-5FN (Type 39) *massovii* with revised front cowling details.

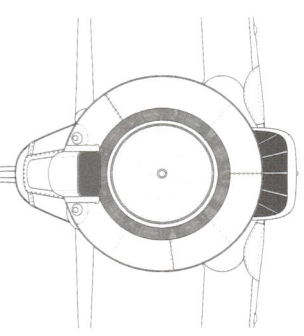

Front view La-5FN (Type 39) *massovii* with revised cowling details.

La-5FN 'late' (Type 41)
Factory № 21, 99, 381

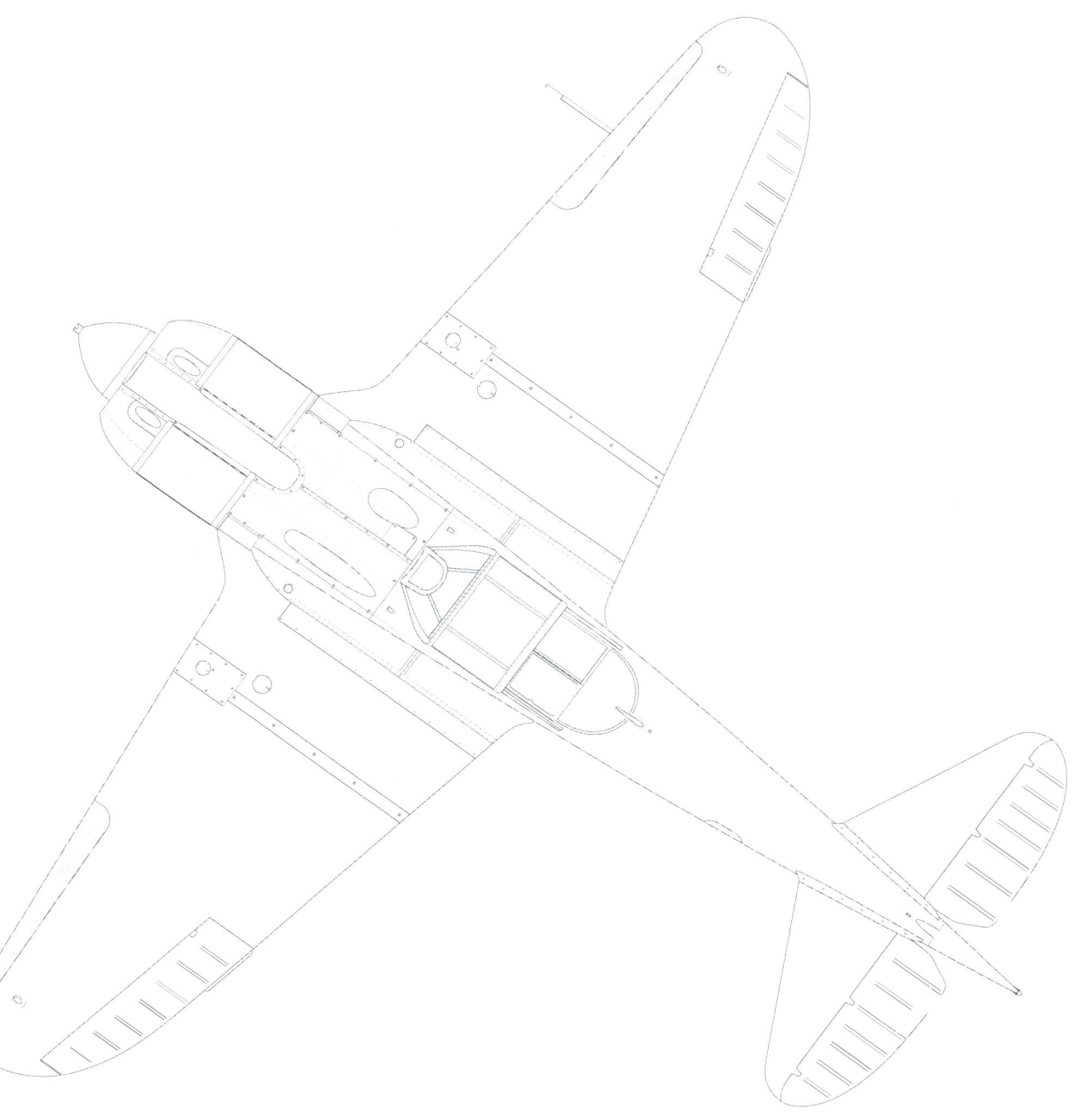

Underside view identical to La-5FN massovii; see page 68
Front view identical to La-5N massovii; see page 69

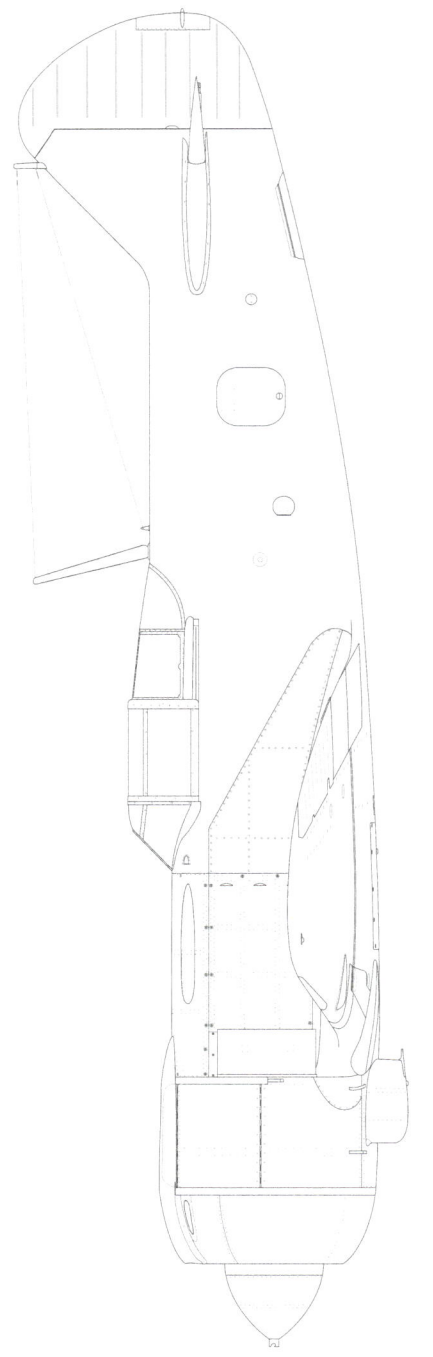

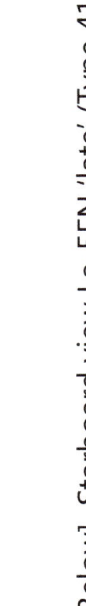

[Above] Port view La-5FN 'late' (Type 41)

[Below] Starboard view La-5FN 'late' (Type 41)

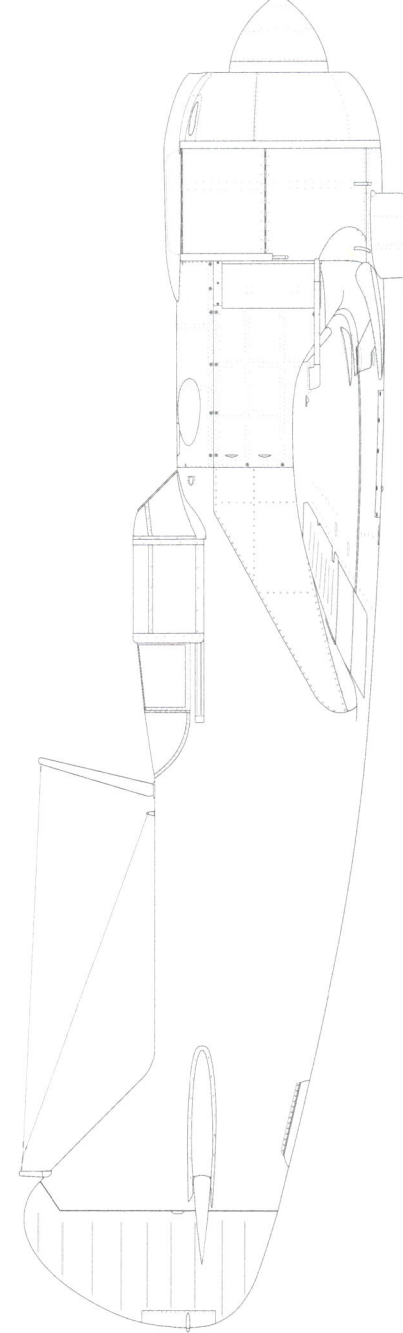

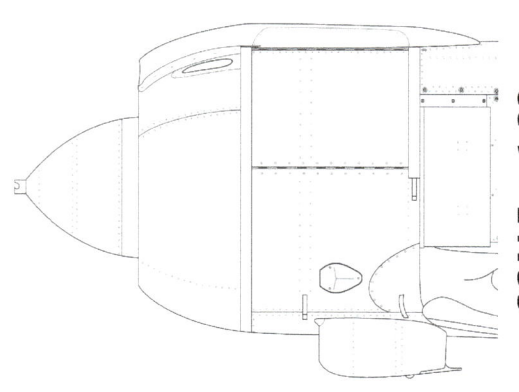

SCALE = 1:33

[Left, Above Centre] This curious cover has been mooted as a modification to some Type 41 examples. This author is not convinced. We know this item only from two photographs depicting aircraft in service post war with a Czechoslovak unit. The author is aware of no other image showing such an item, and certainly not in VVS service. The cover itself is not especially well designed, standing proud of the surface and inviting considerable drag, and does not suggest proper factory type work. Furthermore, this item is not mentioned in the NII VVS' exceedingly detailed report on La-5FN p/n 41210605. As a result, this author suggests that the cover probably does not relate to the Type 41 and instead is simply a local field modification of some kind.

La-5UTI M-82FN (Type 43)
Factory № 167 (Penza)

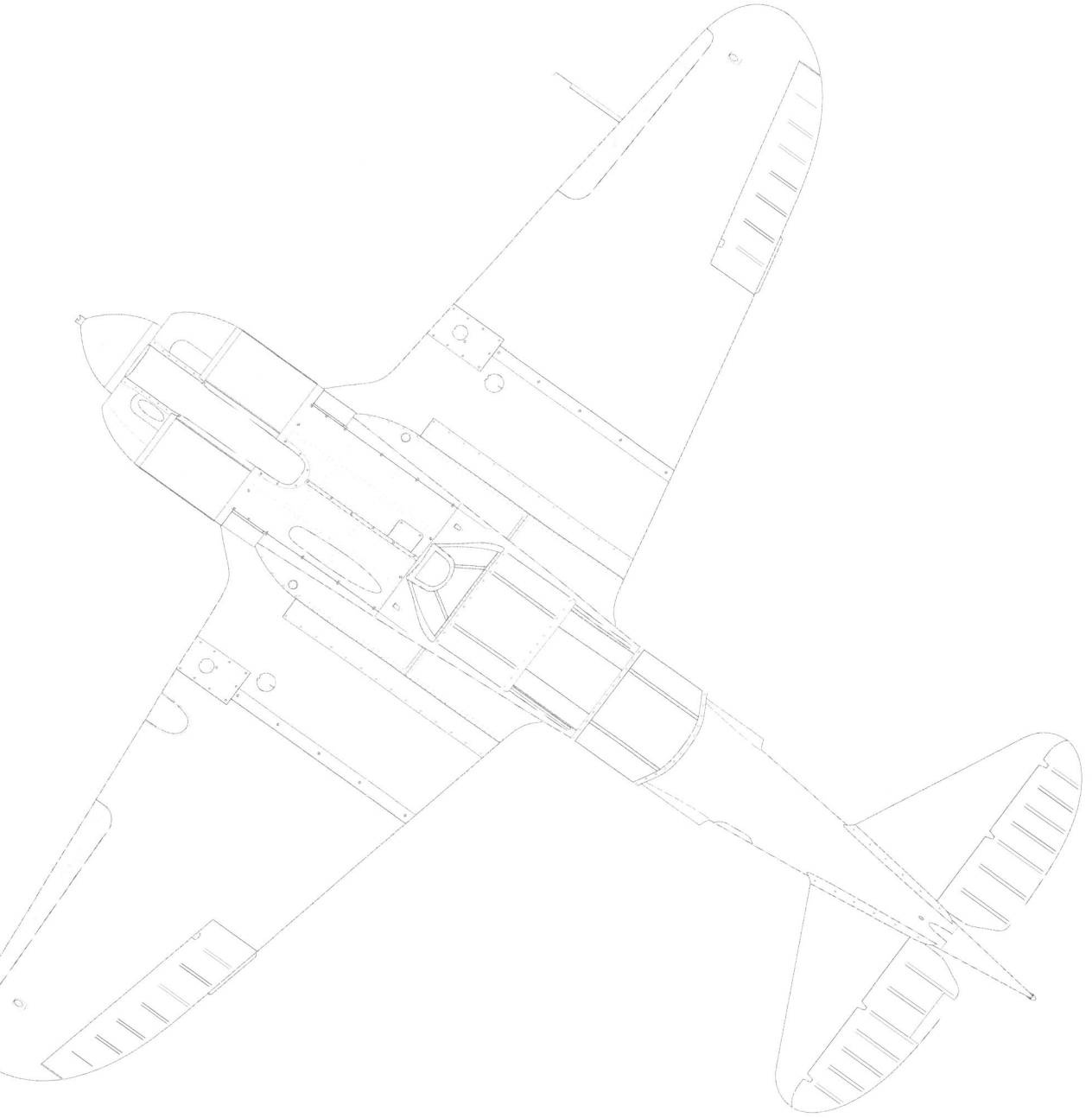

New or notable features in view:
- Central fixed clear canopy section
- Sliding aft cockpit canopy with angled trailing edge
- Rear canopy sliding rails faired into fuselage sides

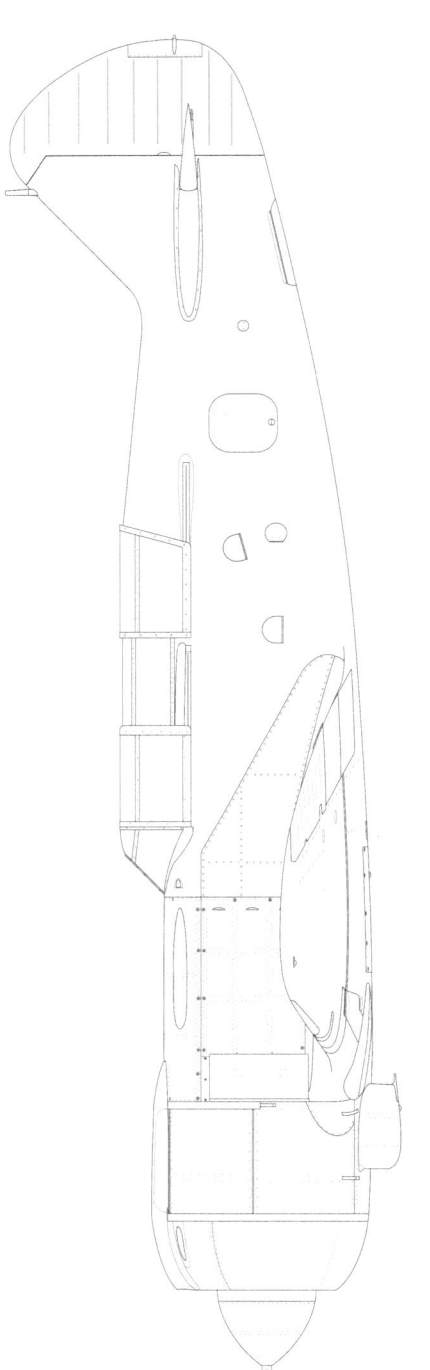

Port view La-5UTI M-82FN (Type 43)

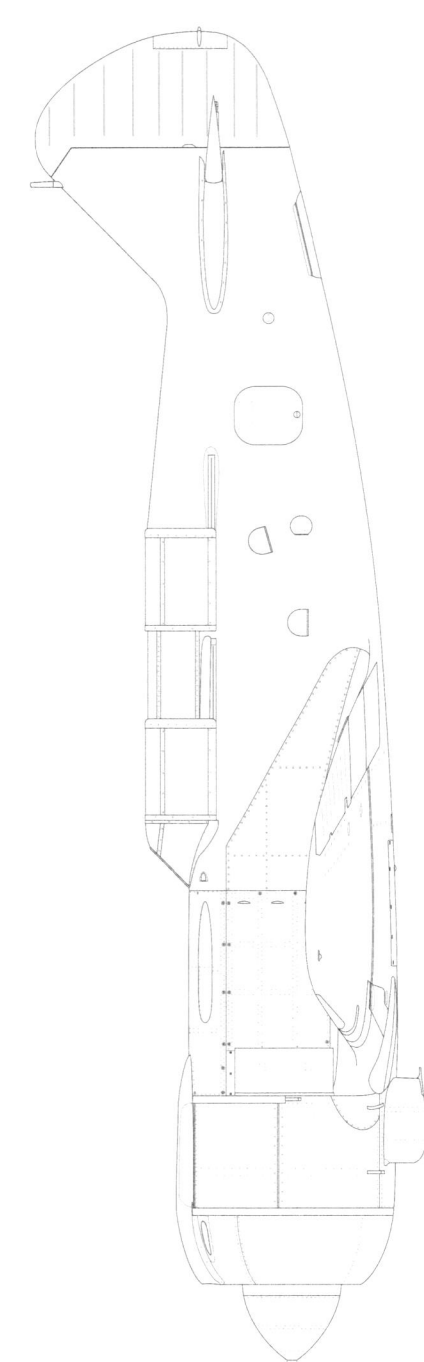

Typical La-5UTI field conversion using the M-82FN motor. Most such conversions utilised a second front sliding canopy unit for the aft cockpit, and the rear turtledecking, entry steps and aft sliding rail fairing could vary considerably in detail.

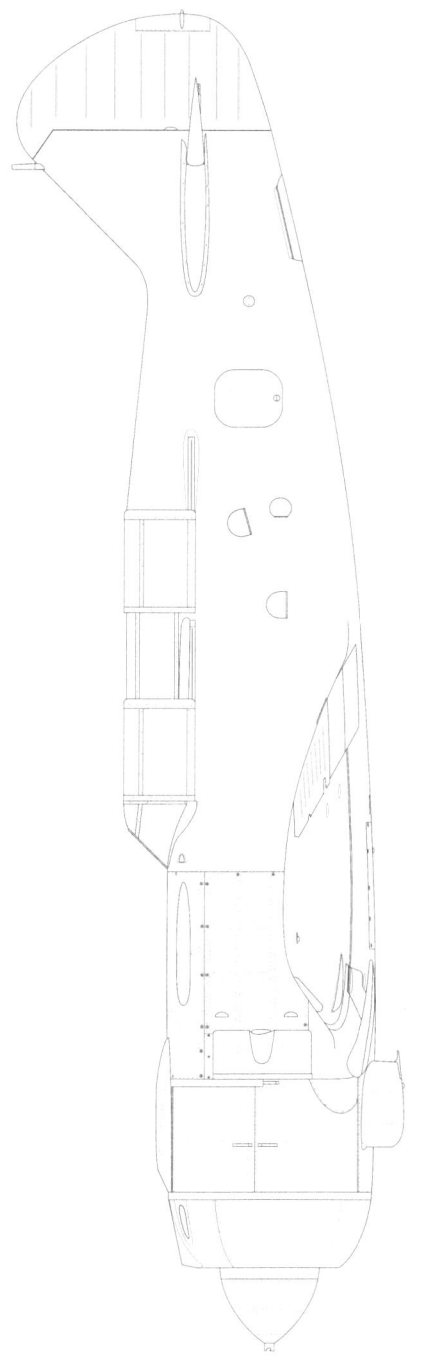

Typical La-5UTI field conversion using the M-82F motor. Most such conversions utilised a second front sliding canopy unit for the aft cockpit, and the rear turtledecking, entry steps and aft sliding rail fairing could vary considerably in detail. Many of these examples were based on La-5F airframes, and in that case the plan-form view would be similar to the La-5F massovii; see page 58

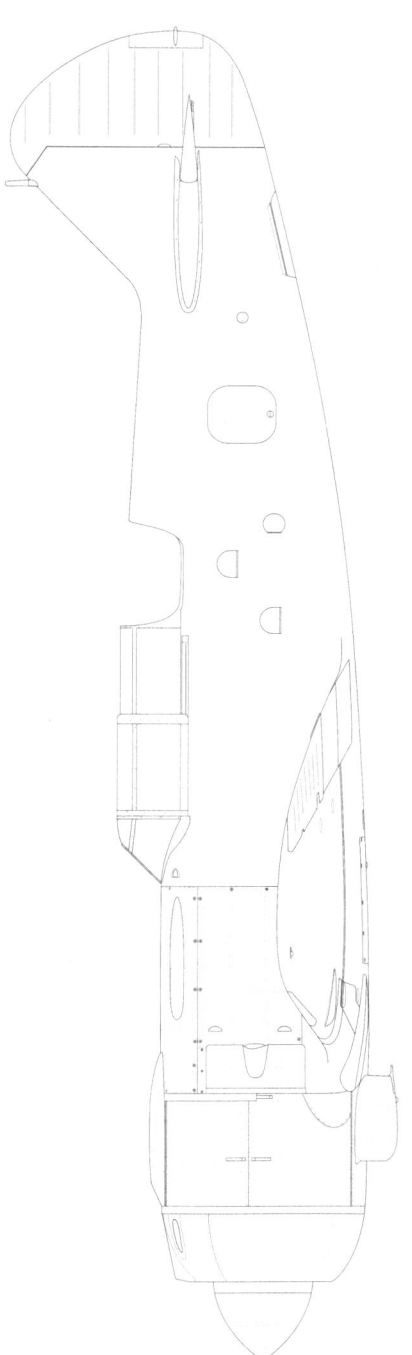

A few La-5F based UTI conversions were completed with an open aft cockpit. These examples were all individually hand built, and no two such aircraft would be identical.

Glossary & Abbreviations

AO (*Aviabomb Oskolochnii*)   Smoke Bomb
Delta Drevesina   A wood-plastic timber product used for primary structural components (e.g. wing spars, etc).
FAB (*Fugasnii aviabomb*)   High-explosive aviation bomb
I (*Istrebitel'*)   Fighter
IAD (*Istrebitel'nii Avia-Diviziia*)   Fighter Air Division, usually comprising four to six Regiments
IAK (*Istrebitel'nii Avia-Kkorpus*)   Fighter Air Corps, usually comprising three to five Divisions
IAP (*Istrebitel'nii Avia-Polk*)   Fighter Air Regiment, usually comprising three to four Squadrons
IAP-VMF   Naval Fighter Regiment
LII (*Letno-Islyedovatel'skii Institut*)   Flight Research Institute
Lt   Lieutenant
KBF (*Krasnoznamennii Baltiskii Flot*)   Red Banner Baltic Fleet
Kpt   Capitan
Maior   Major
NKAP (*Narodnii Kommisariat Aviatsionoy Promishlinosti*)   People's Commissariat for the Aircraft Industry
NII VVS (*Nauchno-Ispitatel'nii Institut Voyenno-Vozdushikh Sil*)   Scientific Test Institute of the Army Air Forces
OKB (*Opitnoe Konstruktorskoe Byuro*)   Experimental Design Bureau
PARM (*Polevie Aviaremontnie Masterskie*)   A forward maintenance and repair workshop
P/N   Production Number (also *Factory Number*; the terms are identical)
PodPolk   Lt. Colonel
SAD   Mixed Air Division
Shpon   A timber product consisting of cross-grained layers of birch strip impregnated with phenol-formaldehyde resin, heat-bonded on one or both sides to bakelite film
TsAGI (*Tsentral'nii Aero-Gidrodinamicheskii Institut*)   Central Aero-Hydrodynamics Institute
UTI (*Uchebno-trenirovannii istrebitel'*)   Fighter-Trainer Aircraft
VMF (*Voenno-Morskoy Flot SSSR*)   Naval Forces of the USSR

Cyrillic Transliteration Method

The new Russian to English transliteration system employed in the Profile & Scale series.

А	Б	В	Г	Д	Е	Ё	Ж	З	И	Й	К	Л	М	Н	О	П
A	B	V	G	D	E	E	Zh	Z	I	I	K	L	M	N	O	P

Р	С	Т	У	Ф	Х	Ц	Ч	Ш	Щ	Ь	Ы	Ъ	Э	Ю	Я
R	S	T	U	F	Kh	Ts	Ch	Sh	Sh	'	Y	'	Eh	Yu	Ya

Appendix I: Photo Fakes

Above we have a somewhat infamous profile which the author completed years ago. As happened so often in those days, the various "experts" of the WWW decried the profile as baseless and fantasy, this on the grounds that "they" (as such) had never seen such a photo. Such complaints-- then as now-- are drivel. This author has *never* completed any profile or other such work without a photographic reference, except in the rare case where a reconstruction is attempted, and work of this kind is *always clearly labelled as such*.

However, it is true to say that this photograph was never *published*. The image was seen by the author in a private collection-- along with many others-- during 2005. In retrospect, one can now understand very well why this image was never published: **it is a fake**. For the time-- more than 10 years ago-- the quality of the digital manipulation seen in this image was very good. Presenting the image on period-looking photo paper made it all the more convincing. The author was taken in, and created this profile. A cropped version of the original image may be seen in *La-5/7 Fighters In Action* on page 12, for comparison

Sadly, the wide-spread availably of exceedingly powerful digital manipulation tools has resulted in an industry of forgeries, of which this is only a single example. Such software is now so good that even *bona fide* experts in photographic interpretation can often be fooled, which alas has led to a very confusing and dangerous situation as regards historical research on virtually any topic.

Appendix II: Cooling Louvres Explained

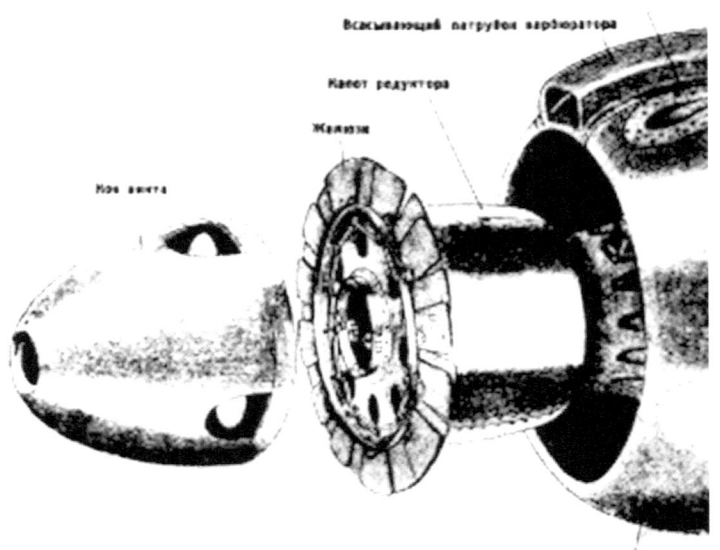

A diagram of the La-5 cooling louvres from the La-5FN Technical Manual (T.O.); the mechanism was the same for all variants. Two rows of roughly square plates are drawn spiralling into the unit, gradually exposing the engine, and resulting in the somewhat 'jagged' appearance of the shutters when partly open.

The louvres have just started to retract in this view of an La-5FN.

[Left] The cooling louvres shown in roughly the 2/3 open position (or thereabouts). This is the classic 'saw-tooth' appearance which has been seen in countless profiles of Lavochkin fighters over the years.

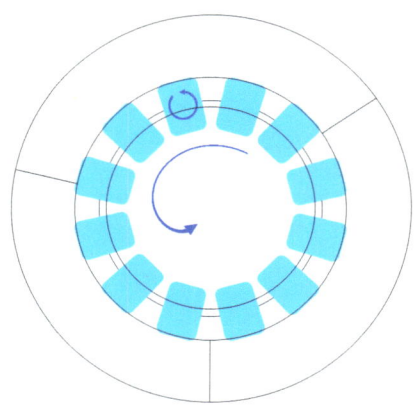

[Left] The front row of shutters shown in their starting position when fully closed. The front row louvres rotated **anti-clockwise** (as seen from the front), and were drawn inwards towards the centre of the mechanism's hub as they did so. In addition, the shutters rotated anti-clockwise about their own axis during this retraction through something like 80° when fully open.

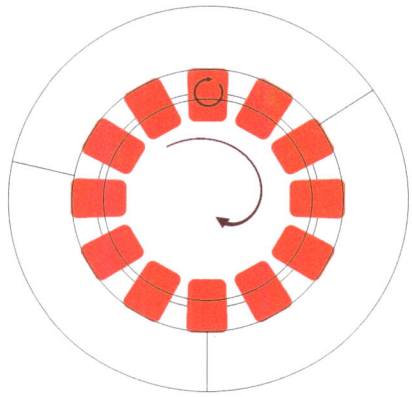

[Left] The back row of shutters shown in their starting position when fully closed. The back row louvres rotated **clockwise** (as seen from the front), and were drawn inwards towards the centre of the mechanism's hub as they did so. In addition, the shutters rotated clockwise about their own axis during this retraction through something like 80° when fully open.

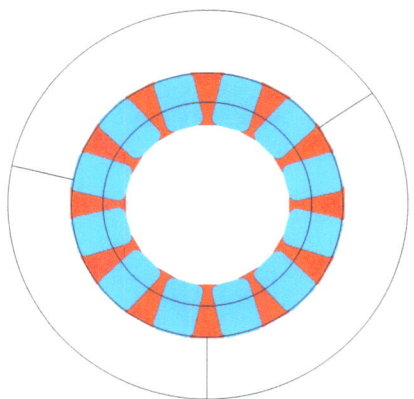

[Left] Both sets of shutters in their starting position when fully closed.

[Right] The double row of shutters is shown well in this lovely image of a colourful La-5F. The cooling louvres here are in the fully closed position.

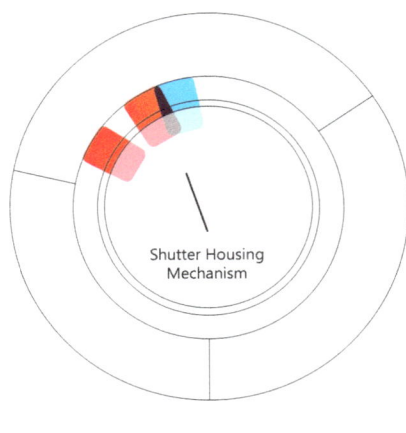

[Left] This diagram shows one shutter from the front row (blue) and two shutters from the back row (red) in their respective starting positions. The central area is the louvre hub mechanism, with the shutters desaturated in this area to show their placement within the unit. The dark colour on the shutters indicates where they overlap, front to back.

[Left] The shutters are starting to open, and the position shown is roughly 1/3 fully open. By this point all of the shutters have rotated 30° (front anti-clockwise, rear clockwise), in addition to having been partly retracted into the hub.

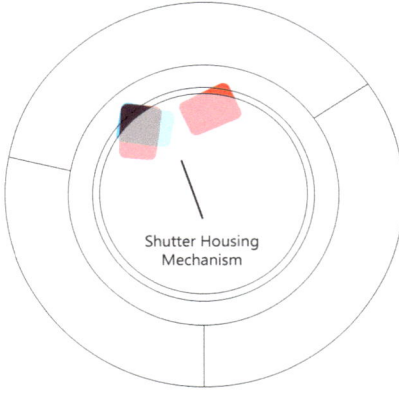

[Left] The shutters are now roughly 2/3 fully open. By this point all of the shutters have rotated 65° (front anti-clockwise, rear clockwise), in addition to having been largely retracted into the hub.

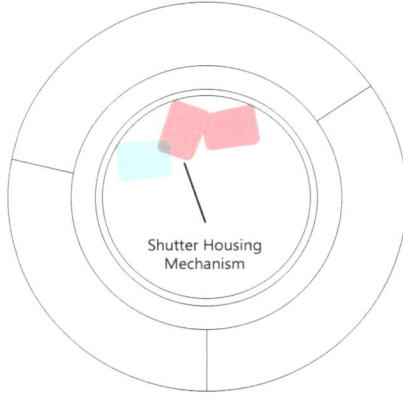

[Left] The shutters in their fully open position. All of the shutters have rotated through 80° (front anti-clockwise, rear clockwise), and have been retracted into the hub.

Appendix III: Gor'ki Camouflage

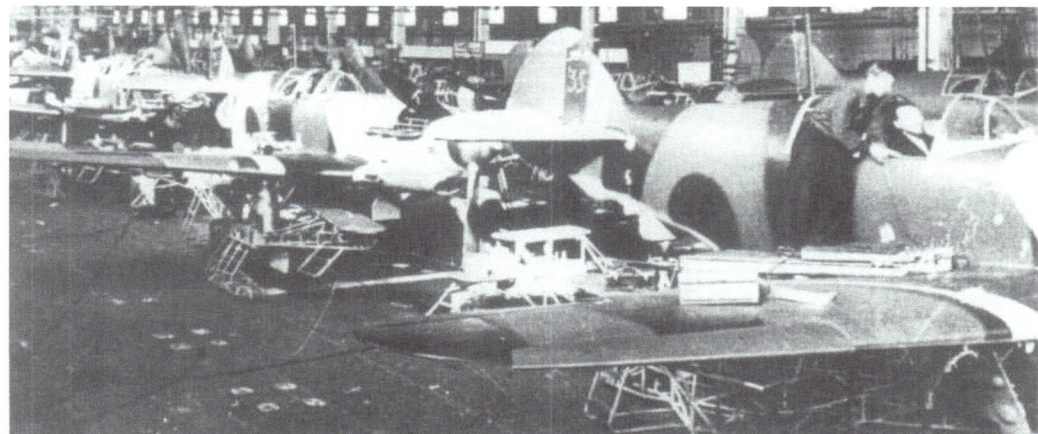

LaGG-3 fighters on the production lines at Factory № 21, Gor'ki, 1942. The 1942 style of the Gor'ki finish is evident, and both two- and three-band examples are in view.

During the late autumn and winter months of 1941, Factory № 21 at Gor'ki was chosen to work in partnership with a new aviation paints factory, № 36 *Aehrolak* in Moscow. This new facility was meant to develop and distribute a new type of aviation lacquer known as *AMT* (literally, "Aviation Matte Finish"). AMT paints were formulated to be effective over all surfaces, and indeed could even be applied without surface priming. Limited numbers of LaGG-3 aircraft were finished with these lacquers during 1941, but the switch to winter colouration (MK-7 White, in several variants) interrupted this process to a degree.

However, when the application of temperate camouflage resumed in the spring of 1942, Factory № 21 had *completely* converted to the use of AMT finishes. Following this development, a new uniform camouflage pattern appeared at the factory for use on both the LaGG-3 and La-5 programs. This pattern has been identified by several names, including the "Gor'ki Standard Pattern", the "Gor'ki Template", the "Gor'ki AMT Scheme", and probably several more besides. Be that is it may, whatever name one chooses to use for the pattern, its fundamental properties are now clear, and illustrated in the following schematics. The colouration in all cases is *AMT-4 Green* and *AMT-6 Black* over *AMT-7 Blue*.

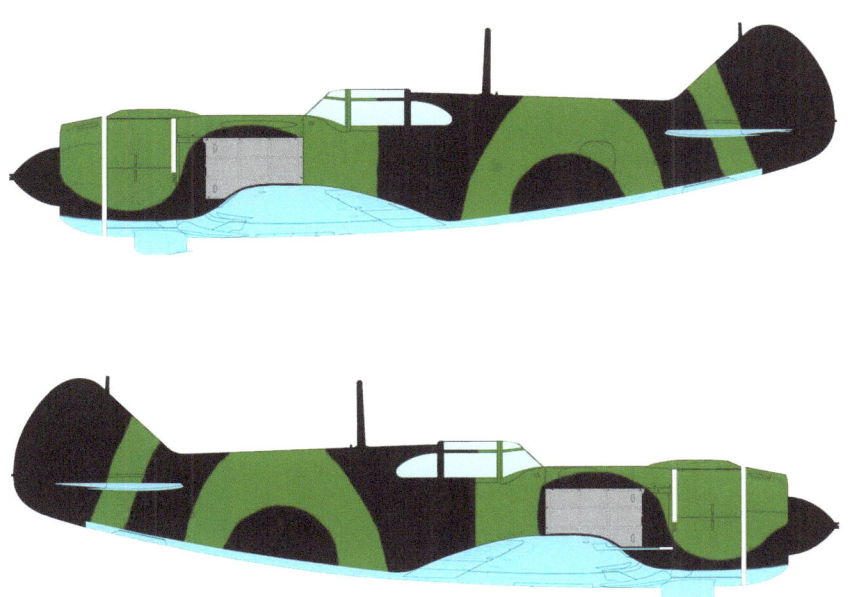

[Left] The initial versions of the Gor'ki scheme were characterised by a nearly symmetrical application, port to starboard. The central 'hump' feature on the fuselage sides was often quite round, and extended almost half way up the fuselage. On the La-5, the cowling application usually covered the stainless steel sheet area, which was often unpainted in factory work. A very low 'swoop' was seen over the cowling, and the spinner was painted with Black. The upper/lower colour demarcation was quite low, extending to the rudder hinge line. Obviously, these diagrams show a typical such scheme; individual permutations and variations were commonplace.

[Left] A top side view of the initial Gor'ki scheme. This is the three-band application, in which three distinct areas of Black colouration were seen on each wings, these applied in rough bands.

[Left] Here is the two-band application of the same Gor'ki pattern. The upper surface colour demarcations were seen in various degrees of hardness, from somewhat sharp [Above] to semi-soft, as shown here.

During 1943 production, the trend may be clearly identified for a slight revision to the scheme. The pattern over the fuselage area was a bit 'tighter', that is to say the round 'hump' feature being diminished and the surrounding areas of Black enlarged to fill the space. The 'swoop' over the cowling was often lower, sometimes almost in contact with the underside AMT-7 colour.

[Left] A La-5F *massovii* showing the upper surface view of the 1943 type Gor'ki scheme.

A curious permutation to the Gor'ki style scheme is shown in this illustration. La-5s with this style of finish are widely known during 1942, but from whence do they come? The upper surface pattern is similar to that from Factory № 21, but the fuselage and cowling feature distinct and consistent differences-- a broad central 'hump' feature, abbreviated cowling application, and Black colour only along the fin/rudder leading edge. Does this scheme denote the work of Factory 381, perhaps? This facility built very few Type 37 examples, to be sure, but then why are they so consistently unique if from Gor'ki?? At the time of writing the mystery is not solved, and we can only hope that soon new information will come to light on this fascinating point.

Lightning Source UK Ltd.
Milton Keynes UK
UKHW020948301219
356015UK00003B/5/P